THE STATES AND HIGHER EDUCATION

A Proud Past and a Vital Future

A COMMENTARY OF THE CARNEGIE
FOUNDATION FOR THE ADVANCEMENT
OF TEACHING

A Commentary of The Carnegie Foundation for the Advancement of Teaching

THE STATES AND
HIGHER EDUCATION

*A Proud Past and
a Vital Future*

Jossey-Bass Publishers

San Francisco · Washington · London · 1976

THE STATES AND HIGHER EDUCATION
A Proud Past and a Vital Future
The Carnegie Foundation for the Advancement of Teaching

Copyright © 1976 by: The Carnegie Foundation
for the Advancement of Teaching

Jossey-Bass, Inc., Publishers
615 Montgomery Street
San Francisco, California 94111

Jossey-Bass Limited
44 Hatton Garden
London EC1N 8ER

*This report is issued by The Carnegie Foundation for the Advancement
of Teaching with headquarters at 437 Madison Avenue,
New York, New York 10022.*

*Copies are available from Jossey-Bass, San Francisco,
for the United States, Canada, and Possessions.
Copies for the rest of the world are available from
Jossey-Bass, London.*

Library of Congress Catalogue Card Number LC 76-011958

International Standard Book Number ISBN 0-87589-282-5

Manufactured in the United States of America

DESIGN BY WILLI BAUM

FIRST EDITION

Code 7610

The Carnegie Council Series

The Federal Role in Postsecondary
Education: Unfinished Business,
1975-1980
*The Carnegie Council on Policy
Studies in Higher Education*

More than Survival: Prospects
for Higher Education in a
Period of Uncertainty
*The Carnegie Foundation for
the Advancement of Teaching*

Making Affirmative Action Work
in Higher Education: An Analysis
of Institutional and Federal
Policies with Recommendations
*The Carnegie Council on Policy
Studies in Higher Education*

Presidents Confront Reality:
From Edifice Complex to
University Without Walls
*Lyman A. Glenny, John R. Shea,
Janet H. Ruyle, Kathryn H. Freschi*

Low or No Tuition: The Feasibil-
ity of a National Policy for the
First Two Years of College
*The Carnegie Council on Policy
Studies in Higher Education*

Managing Multicampus Systems:
Effective Administration in an
Unsteady State
Eugene C. Lee, Frank M. Bowen

Challenges Past, Challenges
Present: An Analysis of
American Higher Education
Since 1930
David D. Henry

The States and Higher
Education: A Proud Past
and a Vital Future
*The Carnegie Foundation for
the Advancement of Teaching*

Contents

Supplement Contents

(Copies of the supplement to this commentary may be obtained for $6.00 each at the Carnegie Council on Policy Studies in Higher Education, 2150 Shattuck Avenue, Berkeley, California 94704)

A. Statistical Tables

B. State Funds for Innovation, 1960-1975

C. Methods of Assisting Private Institutions

D. Actual and Potential Controls Over Private Institutions

E. Proposals to Define Areas of Institutional Independence and State Control

F. State 1202 Commissions and Their Relations with Other State Boards

G. State Patterns of (1) Campus Governance, (2) Coordination, and (3) Association of the Private Sector to Public Policy

H. State Organizational Charts

Preface

The states, and the colonies before them, have been involved in the development of higher education since the founding of Harvard in 1636. This involvement sometimes has been relatively passive and sometimes—as, for example, in the period after the Civil War with the development of the land-grant universities—relatively active. The current period is again one of relatively great activity, particularly with the increasing centralization of the governance of higher education under state auspices and with the greater assumption by the states of financial support for the private sector of higher education. Thus it is an appropriate time to reexamine the role of the states in higher education.

This report looks at the interrelations between the states and higher education 340 years after these relations first began in Massachusetts. This review takes place when higher education is in a phase of continuing but reduced growth; this phase lies between the enormous expansion of the "Golden Age" of the late 1950s and the early and middle 1960s, and the "steady state" that now looms ahead for the 1980s and most of the 1990s. That we see these relations between the several states and the many institutions of higher education as generally effective and productive is implied by our subtitle "A Proud Past and a Vital Future," but we also see many inadequacies and even some dangers as well.

This topic is not a new one to The Carnegie Foundation for the Advancement of Teaching. In the 1930s, for example,

the Foundation sponsored several very influential studies of the states and higher education. Two of these studies were general in nature, as is this current one, and five were about individual states and Canadian provinces.[1]

In some ways, the 1930s and the 1970s are not so far apart:

- "The current financial stringency" was a problem 40 years ago; and so it is now.
- There then existed "a considerable tendency toward unification and singleness of control of state public higher education"; such a tendency also exists now, but in a greatly augmented fashion.
- Some institutions then had been led "to increase their offerings without due regard to the possibility that at some time they might not be able to maintain so expanded a service"; while we speak here of "surpluses."
- Attention was then "called to the variations between the states in certain aspects of higher education" (with 24 tables to prove the point); in this commentary we set forth many "divergent" patterns (with more than 24 tables!).

The recommendations made then and now are sometimes parallel; for example, "the state's responsibility in the field of

[1]The two general studies are: F. J. Kelly and J. H. McNeely, *The State and Higher Education: Phases of Their Relationship* (New York: The Carnegie Foundation for the Advancement of Teaching in cooperation with the U.S. Office of Education, Department of the Interior, 1933). Quotations in text are from Howard Savage's introduction to this volume. D. S. Hill, *Control of Tax-Supported Higher Education in the United States* (New York: The Carnegie Foundation for the Advancement of Teaching, 1934).

Studies on individual states and provinces include: *Education in Vermont* (published as Bulletin Number 7 of The Carnegie Foundation for the Advancement of Teaching, 1914); *Education in the Maritime Provinces of Canada* (Bulletin Number 16, 1922); *Local Provision for Higher Education in Saskatchewan* (Bulletin Number 27, 1932); *State Higher Education in California* (Sacramento: California State Printing Office, 1932); and *The Student and His Knowledge: Study of the Relations of Secondary and Higher Education in Pennsylvania* (Bulletin Number 29, 1938).

higher education pertains not only to publicly-supported institutions but to privately-supported institutions as well"[2] (1933) is a view echoed in this report. But some recommendations are divergent; for example, this present report is highly critical of the tendency toward centralization, but the great theme then was "unified control." The problems are more similar than the preferred solutions are.

The report that follows is divided into two major sections. The first includes commentary; the second is almost wholly descriptive. The commentary has these major themes:

- Higher education in the United States, with its tripartite support based on state, federal, and private sources of funds, has been comparatively effective in both quantitative and qualitative terms.
- Some surplus facilities now exist as a result of the great expansion of the 1960s, but the greater imbalance is in the deficiencies that remain. We provide entirely new information on the deteriorating position, on a comparative basis, of research universities in a number of states.
- The states are, or will be, in a better position to remedy their deficiencies than is commonly supposed, although the capacity of the states varies greatly. We set forth, in this commentary, an entirely new index of the fiscal capacity of the several states.
- Several major problems lie ahead: (1) of how to maintain dynamism without growth, (2) of how to avoid parochialism as the individual states become a greater source of funds and policy, (3) of how to support the private sector while maintaining its independence, (4) of how to get accountability by higher education without stifling it with detailed regulation, and (5) of how to balance the public interest against the need for institutional autonomy in academic areas of decision-making—what should belong to Caesar and what to Minerva? We make suggestions in each of these areas.

---

[2] Kelly and McNeely (1933, p. viii).

The second section is concerned with diversity. An appreciation of this diversity, in its several dimensions, is absolutely basic to an understanding of higher education in the United States. This explanation of diversity also serves as a "report card" on the conduct of the 50 states toward higher education —and not every state gets a passing grade in every subject.

A separate publication, available from the Carnegie Council on Policy Studies in Higher Education, will set forth data that supplement the material in the basic report.

This report is concerned with the states. The Carnegie Council on Higher Education earlier rendered a report on federal action: *The Federal Role in Postsecondary Education* (1975), and plans a subsequent report on the private role. In total, these three reports will have looked at the three major sources of support for higher education. We should note that this report, even more than the one on the federal role, is concerned with traditional higher education and not with all forms of "postsecondary education."

As would be expected in a subject as full of controversy as "the states and higher education," there have been many disagreements in our discussions. This report sets forth the consensus that has emerged over a series of meetings. Some members, however, if they were preparing individual statements, would wish to take somewhat different positions, particularly on the form and amount of state aid to private institutions, and on the preferred mechanism for coordination and regulation of higher education. The positions taken in this report are thus, for some members, more "acceptable" for public policy than they are "best buys" from the point of view of more individual preferences.

We would like to acknowledge especially the assistance of Theodore Drews of the National Center for Education Statistics in making arrangements for special access to computer data and other information, and of Lyman Glenny, director, Center for Research and Development in Higher Education, University of California, Berkeley, for providing data from his survey of recent trends in state appropriations for higher education.

We wish also to express our appreciation to the following

members of the staff who have assisted in the preparation of the factual material: Marian Gade; Margaret Gordon, with the assistance of Ruth Goto and Stanley Severson; Robert Berdahl, with the assistance of Ami Zusman; and Peggy Heim.

Members of the Board of Trustees of The Carnegie Foundation for the Advancement of Teaching

Elias Blake, Jr.
President
Institute for Services to Education

*Ernest L. Boyer
Chancellor
State University of New York

Cecelia Hodges Drewry
Assistant Dean of the College
Princeton University

Robben Fleming
President
University of Michigan

*E. K. Fretwell, Jr., *Chairperson*
President
State University of New York College at Buffalo

Donald N. Frey
Chairman of the Board
Bell & Howell Co.

William Friday
President
University of North Carolina

Robert F. Goheen
Chairman of the Board
Council on Foundations

*Also member of Carnegie Council on Policy Studies in Higher Education.

Hanna H. Gray
Provost
Yale University

Theodore M. Hesburgh, C.S.C.
President
University of Notre Dame

John G. Kemeny
President
Dartmouth College

*Clark Kerr
Chairman
Carnegie Council on Policy Studies in Higher Education

Candida Lund
President
Rosary College

*Margaret L. A. MacVicar
Associate Professor of Physics
Massachusetts Institute of Technology

Sterling M. McMurrin
Dean of the Graduate School
University of Utah

Malcolm C. Moos
President Emeritus
University of Minnesota

*James A. Perkins
Chairman of the Board
International Council for Educational Development

*Alan Pifer, *ex officio*
President
The Carnegie Foundation for the Advancement of Teaching

*Also member of Carnegie Council on Policy Studies in Higher Education.

*Joseph B. Platt
President
Harvey Mudd College

Stephen H. Spurr
Professor of Public Affairs
University of Texas, Austin

*Pauline Tompkins
President
Cedar Crest College

Sidney J. Weinberg, Jr.
Goldman, Sachs & Co.

Clifton R. Wharton, Jr.
President
Michigan State University

O. Meredith Wilson
Director Emeritus
Center for Advanced Study in the Behavioral Sciences

Members of the Carnegie Council on Policy Studies in Higher Education

William G. Bowen
President
Princeton University

Nolen Ellison
President
Cuyahoga Community College

Rosemary Park
Professor of Education Emeritus
University of California, Los Angeles

Lois Rice
Vice-President
College Entrance Examination Board

*Also member of Carnegie Council on Policy Studies in Higher Education.

William M. Roth
Regent of the University of California

William Van Alstyne
Professor of Law
Duke University

THE STATES AND HIGHER EDUCATION

*A Proud Past and
a Vital Future*

A COMMENTARY OF THE CARNEGIE
FOUNDATION FOR THE ADVANCEMENT
OF TEACHING

For state authorities ... "quick to help and slow to interfere" should be their watchword.

> Daniel Coit Gilman, upon his inauguration as president of the University of California, November 7, 1872

More universities have suffered from political indifference than have ever been upset by political interference.

> Terry Sanford, 1967

1

Commentary—
A Proud Past and
a Vital Future

We look back on a past that includes many accomplishments and ahead to a future that can continue a long record of vitality.

(1) The United States, with its tripartite method of support from state, from federal, and from private sources, has developed a system of higher education that compares favorably on an international basis. It provides relatively more student places than other nations (Figure 1)[1] and has supplied more of the new discoveries of high importance in the natural and social sciences (Figure 2). Both quantity and quality have been well served.

(2) Higher education has gone through a period of great expansion, and there are some resulting excess facilities at the present time as measured in terms of the current level of effective demand (Section 3). These surpluses, so defined, have drawn a great deal of public comment. We find, however, no record of general mismanagement, but quite the contrary. The surpluses are in two areas: teacher-training and Ph.D. output. There were enormous demands for more teachers and more

[1]All figures are positioned at the *end* of the various sections. Figures for Section 1 begin on page 22.

faculty members (and scientists) in the 1960s. In the course of meeting these demands, the capacity which was then created now exceeds the demands of the 1970s—and probably of the 1980s and much of the 1990s as well. These surpluses will be costly until such time as adjustments can be made (relatively quickly for teacher-training and relatively slowly for Ph.D. instruction), but these costs are probably in the range of under 5 percent of the total costs of higher education. (The hospital industry is operating at a load factor of about 80 percent.) The greater costs to American society would have been incurred if the teachers and the Ph.D.'s had not been trained in the 1960s; but because they were trained, the "tidal wave" of students was accommodated at all levels of the educational system, and the United States maintained and even increased its supremacy in research. Much was done well. The triumphant responses to the GI "baby boom" and to Sputnik—once grave national concerns —now have some relatively minor continuing costs.

(3) Much remains to be done. Sections 4, 5, and 6 note that many states still rank low in their provisions of student places, in support of their public institutions of higher education, and in provision of aid to their private institutions. They also show that some states have recently reduced their real levels of support in general and for their research universities in particular. In Section 3, we note some specific areas where deficits still exist—areas of great importance for social policy, particularly for provision of greater equality of opportunity and of better health care training.

Overcoming these deficiencies and deficits (and deficiencies and deficits in federal support levels as well) will be costly. The costs can be met, however, probably over the next decade and certainly over the remainder of this century, without any rise, and possibly even with a small decline, in the percentage of the gross national product (GNP) now being spent on higher education. This estimate assumes that the GNP rises at least 2.5 to 3.5 percent a year in real terms. (Since World War II it has risen at a rate of over 3.5 percent, and the federal administration is now predicting a roughly 6 percent rate for the next five years.) Enrollments will not rise much, if at all, over the

decades ahead, and thus leeway is created by a rising GNP to overcome deficiencies and deficits. As of 1974-75 current-funds expenditures of institutions of higher education were about 2.4 percent of GNP and could fall to 2.0 percent by the year 2000 even with enrollment on a "universal access projection basis."[2] The difference between 2.0 and 2.4 creates possibilities for accommodating improvements—if the national desire to do so exists.

(4) Both the capacity and the desire to undertake improvements are now in doubt. We shall comment here only on the capacity and desire at the state level, leaving aside the equally important federal and private areas of support.

Many states are now in financial difficulty. This results, among other things, from:

- The impact on their resources of the recession and then the depression of the first half-decade of the 1970s
- The rising costs, during the recession and the depression, of welfare
- The longer-term rise in expenses for health and welfare and for other social benefits
- The impact of fast-rising wage and salary and fringe benefit costs in public employment as compared with the private sector

The current crisis, however, will not necessarily continue into the indefinite future:

- The depression is lifting and this simultaneously increases revenues and reduces welfare costs.
- Rises in social welfare benefits seem to have reached something of a plateau, both because the most urgent needs have

---

[2]Carnegie Foundation for the Advancement of Teaching, *More than Survival* (San Francisco: Jossey-Bass, 1975). The actual projection in *More than Survival* was 1.8 percent, but final current-funds expenditures in 1974-75 turned out to be considerably higher than the projected expenditure figure of the U.S. National Center for Education Statistics, which was used in that earlier estimate.

often now been met and because of public resistance to further improvements.

• Rises in state personnel costs may also have reached a plateau, both because private levels have been matched (and in some cases exceeded, particularly when fringe benefits are taken into account) and public resistance has intensified.

• Enrollments in primary and secondary education are now stabilizing or even falling, and expenditures in these areas are, to some extent, competitive with higher education.

• The federal government has taken over some welfare costs (for aged, blind, disabled persons) and may take over more. It has also introduced revenue-sharing and may increase its contributions.

We recognize that the states may incur new costs for day-care centers, correction of pollution, prison improvement, equalization of expenditures in primary and secondary schools, and in other areas; and that tax cuts are more and more appealing politically. We recognize also that different states are in quite different fiscal conditions: some have serious problems of fiscal capacity while some are in a considerably more favorable position. We have compiled a new index of state fiscal capacity by combining, on an equal weighting basis, the influences of the level of per capita income, of level of unemployment, and of the degree to which tax resources have already been utilized (Figure 3). Calculated on this basis, Vermont (and certain other New England states) suffer substantial incapacity and North Dakota (and certain other western states) are in comparatively good shape.

The situation among the states is both very dynamic and very complex. However, the prevailing gloom of today does not necessarily presage doom tomorrow. We believe, on balance, that many, and perhaps most, states will have improved capacity to support higher education in the near future as compared with the current moment and the recent past. However, there can be no certainty about this.

Desire is another matter. We cannot estimate it for the future—personal and public priorities do, and even must, shift very substantially over time. We do note, however, that:

- State expenditures on higher education, in terms of percentage of personal income, have risen substantially historically during both good times and bad (Figure 9, Section 2).
- The percentage of state revenues spent on higher education has, on the average, remained quite steady through some very difficult years (*Supplement,* A-16).
- Enrollments have been maintained, even increased recently, when many analysts were predicting drastic declines. This indicates that social demand for higher education, while shifting in its composition, remains high and is not tied to returns in the labor market on anything like a one-to-one relationship. And state support historically has been enrollment-driven.
- Recent polls indicate that a high public valuation is placed on education[3] and this valuation presumably has some impact on the democratic political process.

Five Concerns

Dynamism. Higher education in the United States has grown throughout most of its 340 years. Now it faces a quarter of a century of little growth or no growth in enrollments for the first time in history. Yet most progress has come in periods of rapid growth. In two decades, 1870 to 1880 and again in 1960 to 1970, enrollments have doubled and also the greatest advances have been made.

From 1870 to 1880, the first large-scale study of the natural sciences, engineering, and agriculture was introduced into American higher education, and, in the process, a strong research component was introduced. Universities began to encourage service activities, utilizing the growing number of research

[3] A study recently released by Gallup International, based on a survey in June 1975, shows the public's top priorities (for federal spending) to be "health care, public school education and law enforcement." (George Gallup, "Poll Tells What Public Wants Most," San Francisco *Chronicle,* February 5, 1976, p. 11.)

A Louis Harris poll taken in March 1976 indicates that higher education ranks second only to medicine in the public confidence in leadership of societal institutions, although confidence in all institutions has declined in recent years. (San Francisco *Sunday Examiner & Chronicle,* March 28, 1976, p. A-3.)

scientists. An ideal of academic freedom evolved, an ideal almost unknown to pre-Civil War colleges and universities. Higher education started moving toward broader access for students instead of the much more limited access prior to that time. This was also a period of great change in governance. Growth brought into positions of importance the presidents who became the giants of the period—Charles W. Eliot of Harvard, Andrew D. White of Cornell, James B. Angell of Michigan, and many others. That period also bred a new type of trustee, a person drawn from the community at large rather than from a religious institution, a person more aggressively committed to tying the university to the needs of an expanding society—a modern trustee. That was a decade of signal educational improvement in the course of a fantastic growth.

As for the decade of the 1960s, it is sometimes said that no change took place, that higher education just doubled what it was already doing. That, of course, is not true. During the 1960s, the community college movement developed clear across the country, far beyond the earlier concentrations in Florida, California, and a few other states. That movement represented an enormous change and, overall, an enormous improvement in the provision of tertiary education for the American people. The sixties witnessed a great extension of science into entirely new areas; significant developments took place in the relatively new fields of biochemistry and biophysics, for example. It was also during this period of growth that higher education broke through the restrictive policies of the American Medical Association and the state medical associations, which sought to limit the numbers of medical students in individual classes. By breaking through these barriers, and by nearly doubling the number of medical doctors produced in the country, higher education largely overcame what had been a strong monopoly. In the sixties, there were new experiments in the development of cluster colleges throughout the country, including Michigan State University and the Santa Cruz and San Diego campuses of the University of California. In many states, teachers colleges were transformed into comprehensive colleges and universities. Another development of the sixties was the initiation of the

movement toward universal access—the United States was the first nation in the world to try to provide a place for every young person in the country who wanted to attend a third-level institution.

The next decade of substantial growth will be from 2000 to 2010. This will be a very special period for higher education, and those interested in innovation and improvement and dynamism might well wish that the intervening 25 years would disappear. In that first decade of the coming century, at least 40 percent of college and university faculties will be replaced. More than half of all present faculty members were hired in the 1960s, and they will be retiring mostly during the years 2000 to 2010; the opportunity of replacing 40 percent or more of all university faculty in one decade creates enormous possibilities for changing programs, introducing new disciplines, and setting new priorities.

Of all university building space existing today, 55 percent was constructed in the 1960s; it will be extremely difficult to create new plant until these buildings live out their 30- to 40-year period of usefulness. So, after the year 2000, about one-half of higher education facilities will have to be rebuilt or remodeled. This is not the year 2000, however, and we can only hope to make the best of the situation in which we find ourselves.

Just as most biological mutations are regressive, or at least nonviable, change is not always for the better; often it is for the worse. But the difficulty of change in higher education, as in the biological world, would reduce adaptability to new circumstances and the chances for improvement even if circumstances do not change. Thus it is important that opportunities for new developments be kept open even in a period when growth no longer provides an easy opening for their introduction. Many experiments will, of course, fail, as they should, but some will meet the tests of academic scrutiny and of budgetary review for cost effectiveness.

The preservation of dynamism is mostly up to the institutions themselves, but the policies of the states can help by:

- Providing state funds to support innovations, as is now done at the federal level through the Fund for the Improvement of Post-Secondary Education (FIPSE) and by some states (see *Supplement,* Section B, for a listing of state funds for innovation). The most popular program thus far encouraged by state support has been improvement of instruction.
- Encouraging institutions, in the course of the budget-making process, to set aside 1 to 3 percent of existing funds each year, by curtailing old activities, for use in new endeavors.
- Preserving the private segment of higher education, which historically has been the more open to innovation and the more responsive to new situations, as some private campuses are today. Some of the less prestigious of these institutions are currently showing the greater initiative in making changes. Changes now occur more on the periphery than at the core.
- Encouraging, with financial support, the introduction of the new technology in instruction.
- Avoiding undue rigidity in state formulas for financial support which impede or prevent new approaches of promise.
- Halting the spread of more and more detailed controls that discourage constructive leadership at the campus level.

Parochialism. An increasing tendency to advance the "new parochialism" concerns us. It shows up in many ways:

- Higher and higher out-of-state tuition charges as compared with in-state charges
- Restriction of state scholarships to use at in-state institutions
- Quotas on the number of out-of-state students that can be admitted, as in Michigan, Texas, Virginia, and Wisconsin, among other states
- Federal graduate fellowships distributed to individual institutions rather than to students who can take them where they choose
- Pressures to distribute federal research funds on the basis of geography rather than on merit alone
- The reduction of exchange provisions for students and faculty members going abroad or coming from abroad

• Setting professional examinations (as for the bar) so as to
  favor locally trained persons.

We oppose these tendencies. We favor freedom of choice for
students and scholars that is unimpeded to the maximum extent
reasonably possible by geographical boundaries. Such freedom
adds to the competition among states, among scholars, and
among institutions. It also adds to understanding of, and usually
also to tolerance for, different areas, different institutions, different approaches. The life of the mind should be open to cos-
mopolitan influences.

Solutions are not easy to find. They rely on self-denial of
parochial tendencies by the states (as by Pennsylvania in the
award of scholarships), on regional compacts (as through the
Southern Regional Education Board), on careful attention by
the federal government to its own direct programs, and on federal encouragement of interstate mobility in its joint programs
with the states. We particularly urge the federal government to
require the states to allow some reasonable portability of grants
under the State Student Incentive Grant (SSIG) program.

Preservation of the private sector. The private sector provides
about one-fifth of all student places, about one-half of the
highest quality graduate training and research, much of the diversity within higher education, and special opportunities for
innovative experiments (Section 6).

More than three-fifths of its institutional support comes
from private sources, as against one-fifth for public institutions
(Figure 6). It also receives somewhat more federal funds than its
proportion of total enrollments—42 percent of federal research
and development funds and 33 percent of Supplementary
Opportunity Grants going to nonprofit institutions of higher
education. At the state level, however, it receives only about 4
percent as much money as public institutions. Were it not for
substantial private and federal support, much of the private
sector would be in severe difficulty; some of it is now, even
with access to these sources of support.

The states are already aiding the private sector in many

ways (*Supplement,* Section C). We believe it is in the interest of the states to assist the preservation of the private sector since it:

- Has special contributions to make within the total system of higher education
- Reduces the burdens on state funds[4]
- Increases the competitive pressure on public institutions for effective performance
- Suggests "free market" standards for salaries paid and for teaching loads

Assistance should be given to private institutions in such ways that:

- The public institutions are not neglected. This means caring first for the basic needs of public institutions. We define *basic needs,* as a rough operational guide, as being no lower than current real support per student, except for very special circumstances.
- The additional fiscal burden in any one year is moderate. This means phasing in support for private institutions on a gradual basis.
- The private institutions remain private. We believe a "peril point" is reached when an average of one-half as much state subsidy, on a per student basis, is given directly or indirectly to support of institutional costs to a private as to a comparable public college. The closer a private institution gets to being supported on an equal basis with public institutions, the closer it gets to being made, *de facto*, a public institution, with all the controls that such a status entails (*Supplement,* Section D).
- The private institutions remain competitive with each other and with public institutions in the student market. This

---

[4]States with 20 percent or more of their enrollments in private institutions spend, on the average, about 1.0 percent of personal income on higher education; states with 10 to 19 percent spend 1.25 percent; and states with less than 10 percent spend 1.40 percent.

favors support on an enrollment-driven basis, not on a lump-
sum or "bail-out" basis. (Students, however, may need to be
bailed out by keeping an institution going for the duration of
an academic year or until all students have received degrees or
are able to transfer elsewhere.) We particularly favor the
granting of portable scholarships to students on the basis of
comparative need.
· Private institutions get funds on as assured a long-term basis
as possible. Otherwise they can be held "on the string" by
political forces and potentially made even more dependent on
political considerations than public institutions with their
long tradition of state support. Favors easily given and easily
withdrawn can lead to political dependency and loss of
autonomy.

The basic rule for the future should be: The states make
the best possible use they can of all higher education resources,
both public and private.

Coordination and control. We note later (Section 7) the overall
tendency toward centralization of authority over higher education—from the campus to the multicampus system, and from
governing boards to state mechanisms. We regret this because:

· It reduces the influence of students and of faculty members
and of campus administrators and of members of campus governing boards—all persons who know the most about institutions of higher education, and are the most directly involved
in their operations. It also reduces their sense of responsibility. The governance of academic institutions should include
an influential role for academics and for those in close relations with them.
· This centralization seems to have had no measurable direct
impacts on policies or on practices. No provable case can thus
far be made that higher education is in any way better because of the centralization, except, where it has taken place,
in the one area of careful advance academic planning for
higher education as a whole. It is, of course, not possible to

know, however, what would have happened in the absence of the centralization that did occur.

• The governance processes are worse. They are more costly, more cumbersome, more time-consuming, more frustrating, and place more power in the hands of those who are the furthest removed and who know the least.

This is not to say that higher education should be allowed to go its own way without restraints. It is subject to many restraints, particularly by the student market and by state budgetary controls (and by the judgment of private donors).

We believe that the best restraint is competition. It is for this reason, among others, that we strongly support continuation of the private sector of higher education to provide competition to the public sector.

The next best constraint is the state budget. We support basing budget actions on the best information, the best analyses, and the best judgment of highly qualified persons. Unfortunately, however, these criteria are often not met in practice. New methods of budget-making, such as performance budgeting, should be experimented with, but we caution that they have not yet proven their value.

These two (and other constraints, such as the operation of the law), however, are not fully adequate. Neither the market nor the budget is a good mechanism for long-range planning. They both respond to more immediate considerations. Consequently, we strongly favor a mechanism to prepare a long-range plan to inform and, hopefully, to improve the decisions made by budgetary authorities, by institutional boards, and by students in making their choices. We believe that advisory councils are the best mechanism for preparing such plans. Their memberships and staffs can be selected for this purpose. They are not tied down by or committed to operating decisions. They are not parties at interest as are consolidated boards and regulatory agencies. (For the distinctions among advisory councils, consolidated boards, and regulatory agencies, see Section 7.) Their success relies solely on the quality of their plans and their reputations for independence and integrity. And, in practice, they

(along with some regulatory boards) have generally prepared the better plans. Some advisory councils, however, have been quite ineffective; and some of the best plans have been made by ad hoc, rather than continuing, agencies. The council, however, has an advantage over the ad hoc committee in that it can advise on the continuing implementation of the plan. A good plan should provide for diversity among institutions, which competition will not necessarily assure and may even tend to eliminate, and maintenance of diversity requires continuing scrutiny.

What is needed is good information, careful analysis of it, and thoughtful judgments about policy so that those with final authority can make better decisions if they wish. The final authority, in any event, for most, and perhaps even all, major actions lies with governors and legislators, with governing boards, and with students. In-between regulatory mechanisms cannot long exercise authority of importance strictly on their own. Thus they are driven either to the exercise of authority on minor matters or to acting as the agent of some more forceful authority that has its own power base. In the former case, weak authority over minor matters can be very intrusive; and, in the latter case, the mechanism becomes a means of politicizing higher education.

We place reliance, then, on an effective market, an effective budget-making mechanism, and an effective plan—and not on detailed regulation.

More specific comments follow:

• We favor the presence of lay boards, with substantial delegated powers, at the campus level within multicampus and consolidated systems, as in North Carolina and Utah. They provide better opportunities for lay board members, faculty members, and students to work together than can be provided at the multicampus level alone. Many decisions, in any event, are best made at the campus level. Also, campus-by-campus diversity is best preserved in the long run with separate local boards to help define and protect it.
• We believe it is unwise to have no planning mechanism at the state level for all of higher education, as is now the case in

nine states (except for the thus far generally ineffective 1202
Commissions). Higher education in all states can benefit from
plans that look at all of higher education together and at the
longer run. From time to time, the entire system should be
evaluated in depth in ways that neither market processes, nor
budgeting decisions, nor legislative actions can do.

• If a state goes beyond an advisory mechanism, which we do
not recommend, we believe it is better to develop a consolidated board than a regulatory agency. The consolidated
board means that basic decisions are made inside, not outside,
higher education, and that higher education has a spokesman
to the state rather than just a spokesman from the state (the
executive officer of a regulatory agency most often reflects
the views of the governor—and may be a member of his cabi-
net—or of one or more forceful legislators, since these are the
power bases of such officers). The president of a consolidated
system has his own constituency of students, staff, alumni,
and friends of the consolidated institution. The consolidated
system can, if it wishes to do so, both make better use of
funds, through avoidance of duplication of effort and insis-
tence upon interinstitutional cooperation, and resolve competition and conflict among institutions and segments with less
intrusion of external politics than any other of the major
alternative mechanisms of governance. Such systems can be
particularly effective during a period of retrenchment.

• Consolidated boards, however, present some inherent diffi-
culties. Operating boards are not usually very successful at
planning. In large states, a consolidated board has a wide span
of authority to exercise and much complexity to accommodate. A large and complex consolidated system requires especially excellent administrative organization and leadership to
make it work well. The consolidated board, in the long run,
may yield to pressures to homogenize functions among institutions and to move costs upward. It may also be better public policy for a state to be able to relate to several competitive
institutions or segments than to one single power bloc. Competition among segments has some of the advantages of
competition among individual campuses. Additionally, estab-

lishment of a consolidated board tends to be a once-and-for-all solution.

• We do not in any case favor a regulatory agency with its own final authority. In practice, staffs of such boards tend more often than not to come from outside higher education. They create another level of bureaucracy between higher education and state authority, and thus serve to duplicate the work that other state agencies, particularly the budget office but also the staffs of the governor and of the legislative committees, already do. Bureaucracy, in any event, inherently seeks to concentrate on details and to protect the status quo. The state budget, made for the state as a whole, is, in the end, the major method of state constraint, and regulatory pressure beyond the budget is usually both unnecessary and unwise. Such regulatory agencies might serve as buffers between higher education and the state, but in practice, rather than heading off attacks against higher education, some have been red-hot pokers pointed at higher education. They also tend to politicize the governance of higher education since they mostly serve as instruments of elected officials.

    We note that some states (North Carolina, South Carolina, and Texas) have, in practice, reduced certain powers of their agencies, but the general direction of movement has been strongly the other way. Regulatory agencies do, of course, vary greatly in the degree to which they regulate, and less regulation is better than more regulation.

• While the movement has been toward more and more regulation by more and more regulatory agencies, this may be reversed. There is much opposition to regulation generally and of higher education in particular. Also, there is an increasing tendency in some states for governors, legislative committees, state budget officers, and their staffs to take over the work of regulatory agencies or to go directly to higher education or to ignore the regulatory agency decisions. This is partly because of improved technical competence at the higher levels of state government, partly because of competition between governors and legislatures for influence and control, partly because of the ineffectiveness of some regulatory agencies, and

partly because of the tactics of institutions of higher education. In some states, also, faculty and student groups are making their own direct approaches to political authorities and
the representation of higher education is becoming frag-
mented. It may turn out, in the course of history, that the
regulatory phase of higher education was coincident with the
transition from fast growth to steady state, and that a new
phase involving more frontal contact and conflict between
academic and political institutions is now emerging.

• We believe that private institutions can relate to higher education more effectively through an advisory mechanism than
through a consolidated board that does not consolidate them
or through a regulatory agency that does not regulate them.
In both of the latter situations, they are, to some extent, out-
siders.

• Each state has a different history, a different structure, a different set of policies for financial support, and, thus, decisions about coordination will tend to be quite various, as in
fact they are. What works well one place may not be satisfactory in another. Each situation has its own unique elements.
No one pattern will work equally well everywhere. And some
flexibility of arrangements for planning and implementation
may be desirable to accommodate changes in situations and
in the nature of problems to be solved. Occasional reexamination of mechanisms should be undertaken.

• We regret that much of the struggle over coordination is
based on power considerations alone—over who gets the
power—and not on which method of coordination will produce the best results for students, for scholarship, for society
at large. Faculty members and local administrators favor
power at the campus level; systemwide administrators at the
system level; regulatory agencies at the statewide level; and
governors and legislators in their offices or their committees.

We believe that the burden of proof should be on the cen-
tralizers and the regulators to demonstrate that something can
be done better through centralization and regulation than under

the constraints of an active market and of a well-made budget and of a wisely drawn long-range plan. The worst conclusion of current tendencies would be if institutions of higher education became addicted to regulation, as have many American industries. Many regulated industries have come to like regulation. They escape the rigors of competition. They pass tough decisions and harsh responsibilities up the line. They become lazy and irresponsible. Some of higher education is still fighting this possible fate.

No system of coordination will be fully satisfactory. The problems are too dynamic and the interest groups too diverse. As states search for a more perfect system, the attempted solution is too often directed toward more centralization rather than less. The better answer, however, might lie in a more active market, a more effective budget, a more wisely drawn basic plan, or a higher quality of staff. Each of these possibilities should be explored before further centralization, with its many attendant problems, is chosen as the one and only solution.

Overall, we caution that the external search for small efficiencies and improvements in the short run may kill the spirit of initiative, the self-reliance and the self-responsibility of higher education in the long run and thus, also, lead to major inefficiencies and to deterioration.

Institutional independence. The independence of institutions of higher education has been eroding rapidly, not just through the new centralization, but also through older mechanisms of control. This erosion, the fastest in history, is at the hands of both the states and the federal government. Our concern here is with the states. Higher education was set up to be an independent sector of our society. The Dartmouth College case (1819) protected the autonomy of private institutions. The states, also, have made special arrangements to protect the independence of public institutions:[5]

[5] Carnegie Commission on Higher Education, *The Capitol and the Campus: State Responsibility for Postsecondary Education* (New York: McGraw-Hill, 1971).

- Twenty-three states give some form of constitutional recognition to higher education, whereas few state departments, other than constitutional offices, are so recognized.
- Forty states confer corporate powers on their highest educational boards (few other departments have them).
- Elections or appointments of board members are for a longer period than for most public offices, and it is often specified that selection of board members be on a nonpolitical basis.
- Many boards have been given direct borrowing power rarely given to state divisions.
- Many are given power to appoint treasurers and select their own depositories and disburse funds, especially institutional funds, directly—a condition very rare in other state agencies.
- Many higher education boards are given wide discretion and, in many instances, complete autonomy on policy matters, such as admissions requirements, graduation requirements, programs, courses, and degrees to be offered.
- Almost all states leave to their higher education boards full authority over all matters relating to academic and professional personnel.

This protection was given willingly, even gladly, for the sake of society, to protect academic life from political interference and from bureaucratic control. Higher education has performed well with this independence. It is ironic that after its period of greatest triumph in meeting the needs of American society for greater access and for better research, it should now be subject to greater control than ever before.

Guerilla warfare now goes on all across the nation over what belongs to the institution and what to the state. Independence erodes yearly in the face of the greater forces in the hands of the state, and frustration on both sides grows daily. We believe that all states should follow the example of the State of Washington[6] and seek to draw up a "treaty" openly and on the

[6] Council for Postsecondary Education, State of Washington, *Planning and Policy Recommendations for Washington Postsecondary Education 1976-1982*, Draft Report, August 1975, pp. 240-242.
The State of Wisconsin now has before it a budget bill (awaiting only the

basis of long-run considerations. There is a revulsion across the nation against needless and unwise controls. We believe this current period of reexamination of regulatory controls offers higher education an opportunity to obtain such treaties. We set forth in *Supplement* Section E some suggested guidelines for such treaties and we believe that the Education Commission of the States is a good mechanism for encouraging such treaties, along with the American Council on Education.[7] (*Supplement* Section D sets forth common controls now exercised over private institutions as compared with controls exercised over public institutions, with the implied warning that what now applies to the public sector may some day, to one extent or another, apply to the private sector as well.)

The governor, in many states, is now the one dominant figure in higher education. We consider this to be an unwise long-term development. We suggest, as a check and balance, that governing boards be structured so that, first of all, governors not be members of them, and, second, that appointments to these boards be recommended through appropriate screening mechanisms and be subject to some form of legislative approval. The governor, with his control over budget and his power of final appointment, will still be a forceful figure but less dominant.[8]

The states with historically the greatest freedom for higher education have also been the states that have developed the most outstanding public institutions. The institutions of higher education in Michigan, in particular, in recent years have fought with great success to maintain their independence. They have

---

governor's signature as of April 1976), with amending language from Senate Bill 755, that would exclude from state audit such matters as: academic freedom, the control of academic programs, degree requirements, the approval of courses and curricula, and the conduct of instructional, research, and service activities.

[7] For an indication of the leadership currently being taken by the American Council on Education in this area, see the letter of January 6, 1976, to members from Roger W. Heyns, president.

[8] For a discussion of these and related matters, see Carnegie Commission on Higher Education, *Governance of Higher Education: Six Priority Problems* (New York: McGraw-Hill, 1973).

gained in academic stature, rather than suffered, as a consequence. They began their fight from the base of responsible
institutional conduct.

Concluding Note

The role of the states in higher education has always been important. Today and for the near future, at least, the states are
taking an even more central place. This is partly because the
issues of today—such as creation of more open access places,
correction of surpluses and deficits, support of private institutions, and development of effective coordination—are concentrated at the state level. It is partly, also, because the federal
government, for the time being, is more engaged in reducing
commitments or completing programs already undertaken than
in starting major new initiatives. We do not suggest that this is
desirable but only note that it is true.

Thus the future of higher education is more than usually
dependent on the fiscal resources, on the interest of the people,
and on the judgment of the elected officials of the several
states. There have been many problems in the past that required
solution at the state level and many good solutions were found.
The current period has its own set of problems. We are con-
vinced that good solutions can, and will, be found at the state
level in the future as in the past. The future can be as vital as
the past is proud.

Figure 1. Tertiary education: enrollments[a] per 1,000 population, 1971
(41 countries with the highest enrollment ratios)

Ratio	Country
43.2	**United States**
31.9[b]	New Zealand
30.2[c]	Canada
18.8	Netherlands
18.8[b]	U.S.S.R.
18.3	Japan
18.1[d]	Israel
17.4	Sweden
17.1[e]	Philippines
15.5[f]	Denmark
15.4[g]	France
15.4	Lebanon
15.1	Belgium
14.4[f]	Australia
14.2	Italy
13.7	Yugoslavia
13.7	Norway
13.7	Argentina
13.2	Finland
12.3[b]	Bulgaria
12.2[b]	Poland
12.0[h]	China (Taiwan)
10.9[e]	Albania
10.8[i]	United Kingdom
10.4	Costa Rica
9.7[f]	Ireland
9.7	Peru
9.4	Germany, Fed. Rep. (includes West Berlin)
9.3	Venezuela
9.2	Iceland
8.9	German Dem. Rep.
8.9	Austria
8.9	Czechoslovakia
8.9[f]	Chile
8.3	Hungary
8.3	Greece
7.6	Syria
7.3	Spain
7.3	Romania
7.2	Egypt
7.1	Switzerland

Ratio

[a]Enrollments in tertiary education in principle include students enrolled in degree-granting and non-degree-granting institutions of higher education of all types (universities, teacher-training colleges, technical colleges, etc.), both public and private. As far as possible, these are total (headcount) enrollments of both full-time and part-time students. Because countries differ in their definitions of higher education, enrollment statistics are not always comparable across countries. (See the sources for additional information on discrepancies in the statistics.)

[b]Data include students in evening and correspondence courses.

[c]Data do not include part-time students in nonuniversity courses.

[d]Data include universities and teacher-training colleges only and are for 1970.

[e]Data are for 1969.

[f]Data are for 1970.

[g]Data include universities (for 1971) and *grandes écoles* (for 1969), but do not include all students in higher technical schools.

[h]Data are for 1968.

[i]Enrollment data for England, Wales, and Northern Ireland are for 1970; enrollment data for Scotland are for 1969. Population data are for 1970.

Sources: UNESCO, *Statistical Yearbook, 1971* (Louvain, Belgium: Unesco Press, 1972); UNESCO, *Statistical Yearbook, 1973* (Louvain, Belgium: Unesco Press, 1974).

Figure 2. Research accomplishments in the natural and social sciences

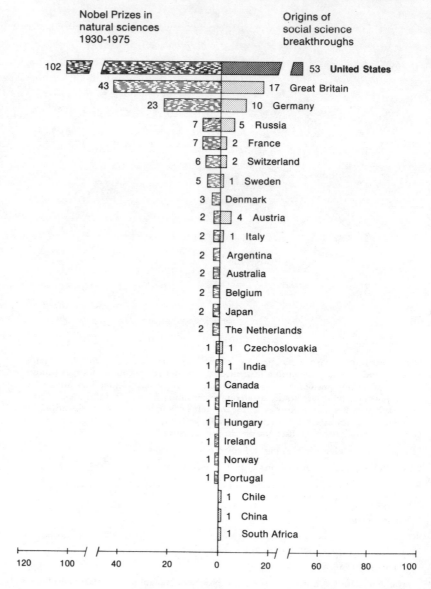

Source: For origins of social science breakthroughs: K. V. Deutsch, J. Platt, and D. Senghaas, "Conditions Favoring Major Advances in Social Science," *Science*, 1971, *171* (3970), 450-459.

Figure 3. Rank of states on fiscal capacity index (high rank reflects high per capita income,[a] relatively large unutilized tax capacity, and low unemployment rate)

States with fiscal capacity greater than or equal to national average (arranged from greater to less capacity)

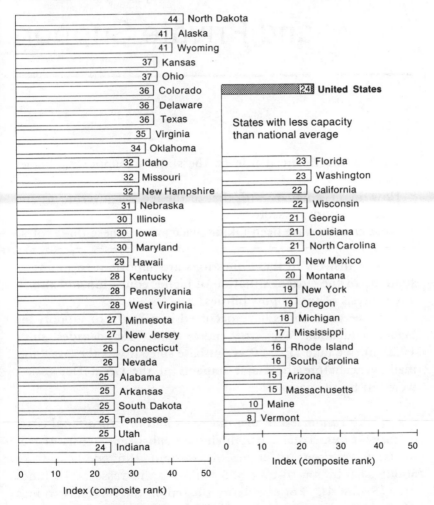

44	North Dakota
41	Alaska
41	Wyoming
37	Kansas
37	Ohio
36	Colorado
36	Delaware
36	Texas
35	Virginia
34	Oklahoma
32	Idaho
32	Missouri
32	New Hampshire
31	Nebraska
30	Illinois
30	Iowa
30	Maryland
29	Hawaii
28	Kentucky
28	Pennsylvania
28	West Virginia
27	Minnesota
27	New Jersey
26	Connecticut
26	Nevada
25	Alabama
25	Arkansas
25	South Dakota
25	Tennessee
25	Utah
24	Indiana

Index (composite rank)

24 United States

States with less capacity than national average

23	Florida
23	Washington
22	California
22	Wisconsin
21	Georgia
21	Louisiana
21	North Carolina
20	New Mexico
20	Montana
19	New York
19	Oregon
18	Michigan
17	Mississippi
16	Rhode Island
16	South Carolina
15	Arizona
15	Massachusetts
10	Maine
8	Vermont

Index (composite rank)

[a]Some states with high per capita income rank low on the index because of heavily utilized tax capacity and high unemployment.

Source: Derived from *Supplement*, A-1.

2

Roles of State, Federal, and Private Support

- What is the financial role of the states in supporting higher education?
- How does it compare with that of the federal government and that of the private sector?
- What changes have been taking place among these three roles?

The answers to these questions are important to an understanding of the current situation of higher education and also to any analysis of future possibilities.

Three great shifts have occurred in patterns of support for higher education over the more than four decades since 1929-30. We take 1929-30 as our base since it was the last "normal" year before the major impacts of the Great Depression were felt by the nation.

(1) *A vast increase in total costs and in educational costs of institutions.* Total costs, including subsistence costs of students, have risen (in terms of constant 1967 dollars) from about $1.6 billion to over $25 billion—an increase of 15 times over (Figure 4). (For calculations based on the forgone earnings of students rather than on subsistence costs, see *Supplement,* A-2.) In terms of the educational costs of institutions (their budgets for educational and general purposes, including re-

search), the increase was one of 23 times over (Figure 5). No such absolute increases in total costs or in educational costs had ever occurred before in our national history nor, in terms of percentage increases, are such augmentations likely to occur again in a similar period. This was, then, a unique period of development.

(2) *A shift from private toward public sources of financial support.* At the level of total costs (including subsistence of students), the private share dropped from 79 to 41 percent, and the public share rose from 21 to 59 percent (Figure 4). (For calculations on the basis of forgone earnings of students, see *Supplement,* A-2.) In terms of the educational costs of institutions, the shift was from 58 percent private and 42 percent public, to 32 percent private and 68 percent public (Figure 5). Institutions then (1929-30) were predominantly private in their sources of support; they are now (1973-74) predominantly public.

The private share, of course, has two major components: current gifts and endowment income, and expenditures by families and by students. The former constitutes about 20 percent of the combined total; the latter about 80 percent. When we speak later of "family" costs, we refer only to the latter figure. The public share, as set forth here, includes only expenditures from appropriations. If what are now called "tax expenditures" (taxes forgone by public entities) were added, public contributions would rise by about $4 billion dollars, mostly from exemptions from property taxes and from income tax deductions. If this sum were added, it would, of course, substantially increase the public share. We have not included it, however, in our calculations.

The United States has always had a mixed system of higher education. The original colonial colleges were, in each case, partly private and partly public, some more private than public and others more public than private. Not until the nineteenth century could it be said, and was it said, that some colleges were "private" and others were "public." But mixtures, at least in terms of sources of support, continued. In 1929-30, the educa-

tional costs of public institutions were met about one-fifth from
private sources, and that percentage continues into the current
period. The big change has been in the financing of private institutions. In our base year, private institutions were supported
only 4 percent from public sources but today 37 percent—an
increase exceeding nine times over (Figure 6). In this sense, public institutions, on the average, continue to be one-fifth private,
and private institutions are by now more than one-third public.

(3) *A shift of public support from state and local toward
federal sources.* In 1929-30 the federal government was a minor
source of governmental appropriations (9 percent), and state
and local sources carried the overwhelming share (91 percent).
Today (1973-74), the distribution is roughly equalized—45 percent federal, and 55 percent state and local (Figure 7). Two
levels of government now are of great significance to higher education where there was only one level before. This carries many
implications concerning the sources of initiative for and the
sources of control over the development of higher education.

Characteristics of Support

(1) *Comparative composition of support.* If we divide support
into three categories—support for institutions, support for research projects, and student aid—we find that our three major
sources of financing demonstrate quite different interests. The
states (and localities) concentrate heavily on support of institutions, the federal government on student assistance and on
research projects, and private sources on student subsistence and,
to a lesser extent, on support of institutions (Figure 8).

This current distribution of attention reflects two great
new developments since 1929-30. The first is the enormous increase in expenditures on research through the universities,
mostly from the federal government. The second is the vastly
augmented public support of students from lower-income families as the nation has moved from selective to mass to universal
access to higher education. Once again the federal government
has been the main source of these additional funds. The states,
by comparison, remain more concentrated in their financial

support on institutions as such, and private sources remain more concentrated on support of students by those families that can afford to support them.

(2) *Constancy and volatility of support.* State support (as a percentage of total personal income, which is a rough measure of "burden") has been largely enrollment-driven (Figure 9). It even rose at first during the Great Depression. Of course it fell during World War II. It has risen quite steadily since then. The recent record has been remarkable. The taxpayer "burden" ran upward right through the student unrest of the late 1960s, the recession of 1970, and even through the first year (1974-75) of the recent depression. The Carnegie Commission on Higher Education once said that state and local expenditures "will have to rise to approximately 1 percent of personal per capita income."[1] The latest figure then available was for 1966-67 and was 0.7 percent. That 1 percent figure has now been exceeded —during a depression period. It now stands (1974-75) at 1.09.[2] It was 1.03 in 1973-74 (Figure 22, Section 5).

Private support has also been enrollment-driven but has not risen nearly as fast as the state share in terms of percentage of personal income (see Figure 10).

Federal support, likewise in terms of percentage of personal income, has risen the fastest of all (Figure 11). It also appears in its totality to have followed a reasonably smooth course (except for the World War II period), but closer examination of its component parts shows great volatility (Figure 12).

[1] Carnegie Commission on Higher Education, *The Capitol and the Campus: State Responsibility for Postsecondary Education* (New York: McGraw-Hill, 1971), p. 114.

[2] The Commission did say that the level would need to rise above 1.0 if the state share did not continue "the slight relative decline expected" vis-à-vis the federal share, but this slight decline did continue. We do not have a figure for 1975-76. It is possible that the level of support has gone down, reflecting the depression during the period in which appropriations were made. From fragmentary data, we conclude that higher education budgets may have been quite adversely affected in at least Connecticut, Florida, Georgia, Maine, Michigan, New Jersey, New York, Rhode Island, Vermont, and Wisconsin.

Federal support is essentially problem-driven. It responded to the end of World War II and the Korean War and the Vietnam War with educational benefits to veterans; to Sputnik with more money for research; to the civil rights revolution with support for low-income students (which is still rising); and, after the initial response, the amount of money that was provided either declined or stabilized as the national concern for such problems either declined or stabilized. This topical approach is reflected in decisions taken by several congressional committees and in programs administered by several agencies—now one and now another committee and agency takes the initiative. There has been no overall, consistent concern for institutions of higher education.

(3) *Shifting burden of support.* If we exclude enrollment as a factor and concentrate on support per student, we see an interesting picture. The net cost of higher education per student to the family (for subsistence and tuition) has actually gone down in constant dollars by about 9 percent since 1929-30 (Figure 13). This is partly because so much of subsistence costs (and some tuition) is now being funded by Veterans' and Social Security benefits, by Basic Opportunity and other federal grants, and by state scholarship programs. Another reason is because more students were in higher-cost private institutions in 1929-30 and now are in lower cost public institutions; additionally, more students now come from lower-income families. During this period, per capita real income has nearly tripled. Thus the comparative burden, per student, on the average family with college students now, compared with the average family with college students then, has gone down by about two-thirds.[3] The net cost for tuition, however, has risen significantly, but still much less than per capita real income—it has gone up only one-third as fast.

For the state taxpayer, the burden, per student, has risen, however, by more than three times over and even more than that

---

[3]Items on which expenditures have risen considerably more (tripled or more), rather than less, than income are: travel, health, communications (including radio and TV), entertainment, beverages, personal grooming, household appliances and owner-occupied housing. See, for example, C. Almon Jr., and others, *1985: Interindustry Forecasts of the American Economy* (Lexington, Mass.: Lexington Books, 1974).

for the taxpayer at the federal level. The family is comparatively better off, and the taxpayer comparatively worse off. The taxpayer has been the bigger and bigger contributor viewed historically. This does not correspond with the common public impression that families have, over the years, been carrying heavier and heavier burdens, on the average, for the higher education of their children. It is the taxpayers who have done that —for children of their own and for the children of others.

This does not mean, of course, that the burden has not been heavy in recent years for upper-income families whose children do not qualify for student aid, and particularly when these children attend private institutions.

Future Prospects

We do not expect that the next 40 to 50 years will duplicate the changes of the past 40 or 45 years. If they did, by the year 2015 or 2020, the educational costs of higher education would be over $400 billion, or five times the present budget (1967 dollars) for national defense. The public share of institutional costs would have long since approached 100 percent and the private share zero percent; and the federal government would have long since taken over 100 percent of all public funding, leaving the states and localities with zero percent. While the future is obscure, we consider these results unlikely prospects however much some might wish them. We consider it more likely that:

- Total costs and educational costs of institutions will rise in accordance with two factors: rising enrollments to the extent they do rise[4] and rising costs per student which tend to rise in the long run (since 1930) at 2 or 2.5 percentage points per year faster than the general cost of living.[5]
- Some continuing shift will take place from private toward public sources of funds, but at a reduced rate.

[4] See our projections in The Carnegie Foundation for the Advancement of Teaching, *More than Survival: Prospects for Higher Education in a Period of Uncertainty* (San Francisco: Jossey-Bass, 1975).

[5] Carnegie Commission on Higher Education, *The More Effective Use of Resources: An Imperative for Higher Education* (New York: McGraw-Hill, 1972).

- Absolute increases will occur in both federal and state funds in terms of constant dollars (the federal government has much "unfinished business,"[6] and the states have educational deficits to overcome, as we shall indicate later); but we do not expect the current balance of 45 percent federal support/55 percent state and local support to be shifted drastically or perhaps even substantially. It might reach a 50-50 level, but it also might drop to 40-60.
- The current major emphases of the states on institutional support (adding more support for private institutions), and of the federal government on research and on subsidies for lower-income students, and of private sources for support of students from medium- and higher-income families will be maintained as a rough division of labor.
- The greater volatility in the components of federal support than in the totality of state and of private support, which usually has only one or two components, will continue.
- There will be some modest furtherance of the historic tendency of families to shift burdens to taxpayers.
- All of this assumes that the economy will continue to recover from the recent depression; that the gross national product per capita will grow on the average at a slower rate than over the period since World War II but will still continue to grow; that the fiscal position of the states generally will not continue to deteriorate and may even improve; and that the total social demand for higher education will continue at about the current rate even though economic returns to graduates in the labor market decline from their high levels of the 1960s.

Overall, then, we see the states as an essential component of our pluralistic system, with particular historic responsibility for the support of institutions as such. We turn next to how they have, in their several ways, discharged their responsibilities. We note once again, however, that their performances, while central, are not exclusive in their impact on higher education. The states are one leg of the three-legged ladder on which higher education stands.

[6]Carnegie Council on Higher Education, *The Federal Role in Postsecondary Education: Unfinished Business 1975-1980* (San Francisco: Jossey-Bass, 1975).

Figure 4. Changes in public and private shares of costs of higher education, including educational costs of institutions and subsistence costs of students, 1929-30 to 1973-74 (in constant 1967 dollars)

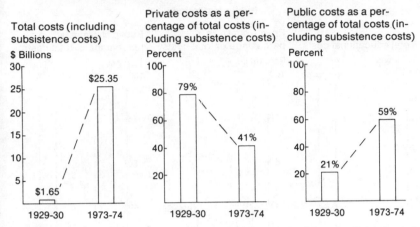

Source: Estimates developed from U.S. National Center for Education Statistics and U.S. Bureau of Labor Statistics data. Estimated tuition and subsistence expenses met from public student aid are allocated to the public share; includes total research funds.

Figure 5. Changes in shares of educational costs of institutions of higher education from public and private sources, 1929-30 to 1973-74 (in constant 1967 dollars)[a]

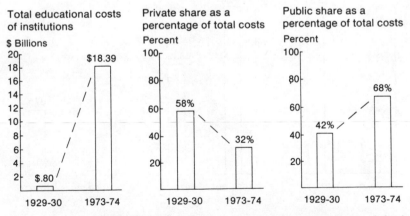

[a]Includes revenue of institutions for educational and general purposes, plus federal allocations for research and development projects. Tuition income has been adjusted to allocate student aid from public funds to the public share.

Source: Estimates developed from U.S. National Center for Education Statistics and U.S. Bureau of Labor Statistics data.

Figure 6. Changes in shares of educational costs of public and private
institutions of higher education from public and private sources, 1929-30
to 1973-74 (in constant 1967 dollars)[a]

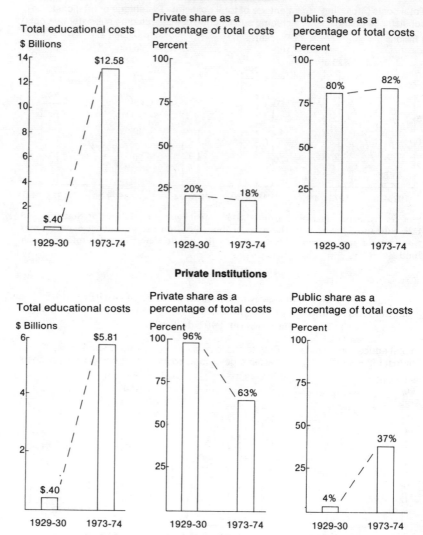

[a]Includes revenue of institutions for educational and general purposes, plus federal
allocations for research and development projects. Tuition income has been adjusted
to allocate student aid from public funds to the public share.

Source: Estimates developed from U.S. National Center for Education Statistics and
U.S. Bureau of Labor Statistics data.

Figure 7. Changes in proportions of total governmental appropriations for higher education from (1) federal and (2) state and local sources, 1929-30 to 1973-74 (in constant 1967 dollars)[a]

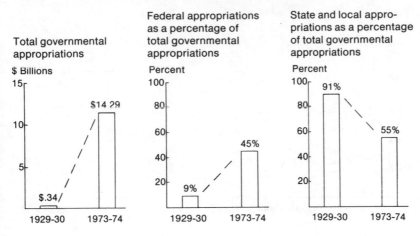

[a]Includes revenue of institutions from public sources plus appropriations for student aid allocated directly to students, including state scholarships and, from federal sources, Basic Educational Opportunity Grants, Veterans' benefits, and Social Security benefits.

Source: Adapted from U.S. National Center for Education Statistics and other data.

Figure 8. Shares of financial support for (1) educational costs of institutions, (2) research, and (3) student subsistence from federal, state and local, and private sources, 1974-75

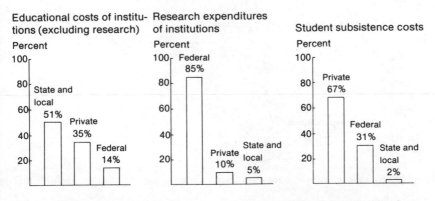

Source: Estimated from U.S. National Center for Education Statistics and other data. Tuition income of institutions has been adjusted to allocate to public sources the estimated proportion of tuition paid from public student aid funds. Similarly, the proportion of student subsistence paid from public sources (including federal Veterans' benefits) has been estimated.

Figure 9. Expenditures of state and local governments on higher education
as a percentage of total personal income, 1929-30 to 1974-75
(biennial to 1973-74)[a]

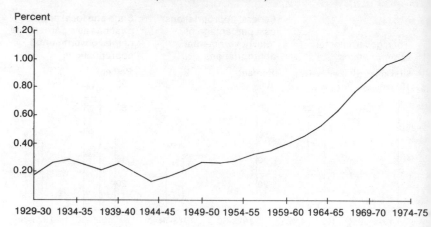

[a]Includes revenue of institutions from state and local governments plus state scholarship funds allocated directly to students. Data for 1974-75 are estimated.

Source: Adapted from U.S. National Center for Education Statistics and U.S. Bureau
of Economic Analysis data.

Figure 10. Tuition and subsistence expenditures of students and
their families as a percentage of total personal income, 1929-30 to 1974-75
(biennial to 1973-74)[a]

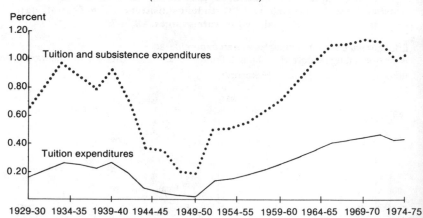

[a]Estimated student aid allocated to tuition and subsistence expenditures has been
deducted, including student aid from all public and private sources.

Source: Adapted from U.S. National Center for Education Statistics, U.S. Bureau of
Economic Analysis, and other data.

Figure 11. Expenditures of the federal government on higher education
as a percentage of total personal income, 1929-30 to 1974-75
(biennial to 1973-74)[a]

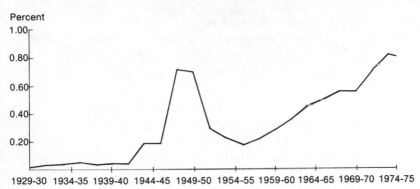

[a]Includes revenue of institutions from the federal government plus student aid allocated directly to students under the Basic Educational Opportunity Grant, Veterans'
benefits, and Social Security benefits programs.

Source: Adapted from U.S. National Center for Education Statistics and U.S. Bureau
of Economic Analysis data, and from data in Carnegie Council on Higher Education,
The Federal Role in Postsecondary Education: Unfinished Business 1975-1980 (San
Francisco: Jossey-Bass, 1975).

Figure 12. Changes in federal expenditures for higher education,
selected items, 1949-50 to 1974-75 (in constant 1967 dollars)

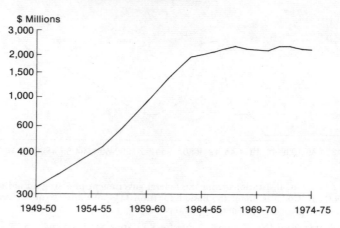

Research funds of institutions
from federal sources

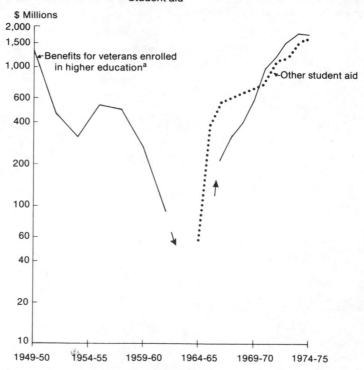

Student aid

Expenditures for graduate fellowships

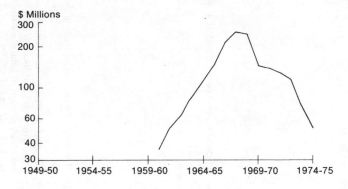

Construction loans and grants[b]

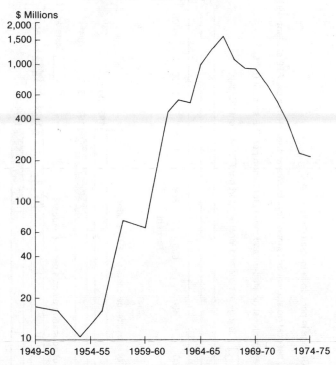

[a]Veterans' benefits fell to $25 million in 1963-64 and to zero in 1965-66.

[b]For the years 1949-50 through 1959-60, data relate to plant-fund income of institutions from federal sources.

Sources: J. O'Neill, *Sources of Funds to Colleges and Universities* (Berkeley, Calif.: Carnegie Commission on Higher Education, 1973); Carnegie Commission on Higher Education, *Higher Education: Who Pays? Who Benefits? Who Should Pay?* (New York: McGraw-Hill, 1973); Carnegie Council on Higher Education, *The Federal Role in Postsecondary Education: Unfinished Business 1975-1980* (San Francisco: Jossey-Bass, 1975); U.S. National Center for Education Statistics, *Digest of Educational Statistics, 1974* (Washington, D.C.: U.S. Government Printing Office, 1975).

Figure 13. Changes in per capita income, student costs, and in sources of financial support for educational and subsistence costs per full-time-equivalent student, 1929-30 to 1974-75 (in constant 1967 dollars)

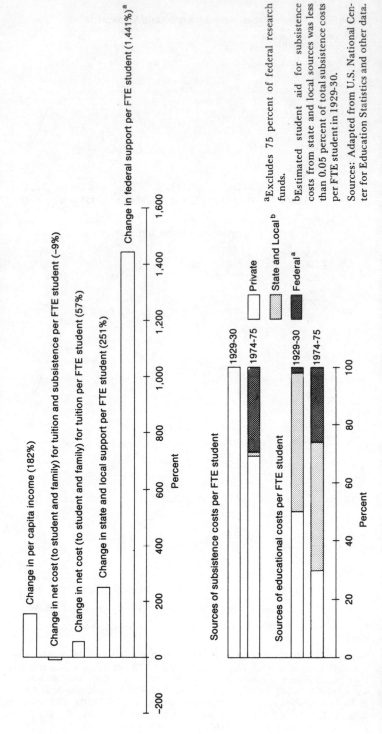

ᵃExcludes 75 percent of federal research funds.

ᵇEstimated student aid for subsistence costs from state and local sources was less than 0.05 percent of total subsistence costs per FTE student in 1929-30.

Sources: Adapted from U.S. National Center for Education Statistics and other data.

3

Surpluses, Deficits, and Special Accomplishments

Surplus capacity is inevitable in a period of suddenly reduced expectations and realizations after a time of vast expansion.[1]

Surplus capacity clearly now exists nationally in:

- Teacher-training
- Production of Ph.D.'s

There is at least a potential surplus of:

- Health Science Centers
- Law Schools

The existence of surpluses has been caused by these general factors:

- The momentum of more than doubling enrollments in the 1960s—sometimes in an almost frantic way to accommodate the "tidal wave" of students—led to some overshooting of actual needs.
- The sudden decline in the birthrate reduced the need for

[1]We define *surplus* as an excess of supply over currently effective demand. Demand could, of course, potentially be raised to match supply if social policy had this as a goal.

teachers—at first at the primary level, next at the secondary level, and subsequently at the college level.

• The slowdown (and even decline for some categories, such as college-age majority males) in the percentage of the age cohort attending college additionally reduced the expected need for college teachers. This slowdown resulted, in part, from recession and depression conditions of the early 1970s and also from the long-term catching up of supply with demand, which has tended to reduce economic returns in the labor market for a college education, compared to returns for a lower level of education. The rising costs of higher education and, for young men, the removal of the draft also played important roles.

• Some aspirations in the 1960s and early 1970s were excessive, and institutions tried to advance themselves—unwisely from a public point of view—by insisting on new medical schools and on new Ph.D. programs regardless of the prospective need for them. Short-term institutional ambition exceeded long-term public need.

• The declining population of many rural areas shifted the locations of need for student places.

• Enthusiasm at the federal level, as in expanding the demand for teacher-training through loan-forgiveness provisions for teachers and in encouraging Ph.D.-training through graduate fellowships and research assistantships and in the creation of new medical schools, greatly added to the impetus toward certain surpluses. The one greatest source of surpluses has been federal initiative.

Only one of the causes for surpluses, excessive ambition, can be laid at the doors of the colleges and universities, and that cause can be placed at the doors of a small minority of the 3,000 institutions—including perhaps 8 that started unnecessary medical centers (sometimes with strong external encouragement), plus most of the nearly 80 that started Ph.D. programs since 1960.

Teacher-training. Surplus capacity exists in many institutions that have concentrated on teacher-training and in nearly all

states. Enrollments in teacher-training programs have gone down by one-half (from 20 to 10 percent of all undergraduate enrollments) and are likely to stay down for a long time to come (for at least 20, and perhaps 25, years).[2] Excess capacity in colleges specializing in teacher-training seems to be particularly concentrated in the following states:[3]

Arkansas	North Dakota
California	Oklahoma
Colorado	Oregon
Georgia	South Dakota
Kansas	Texas
Minnesota	Washington
Missouri	West Virginia
Montana	Wisconsin
Nebraska	

Ph.D. programs. The nation now has the capacity to produce 30,000 or more Ph.D.'s a year—it did produce 33,000 in 1973-74 while still having substantial excess capacity, but the prospective need is more like 20,000 and mostly (80 or 90 percent) in fields that also supply industry and government.[4] About 230 institutions now offer the Ph.D. in one or more fields, although around 100, or at most 150, would be a sufficient number. Seventy-six additional institutions have added Ph.D.-degree programs since 1960—there were 158 institutions offering the Ph.D. in that earlier year.

[2] A recent survey by Alexander Astin shows that the percentage of freshmen students planning to become teachers has slipped from 21.7 percent in 1966 to 6.5 percent in 1975 (*Chronicle of Higher Education*, January 12, 1976, p. 3).

[3] Estimated by finding substantial declines in enrollment in three or more institutions which have historically concentrated heavily on teacher-training.

[4] Our estimate implies a potential surplus of 50 percent. A recent analysis predicts a much greater likely surplus of about 200 percent. New supply is estimated at 583,000 from 1972 to 1985 and openings at 187,000 ("Projected Demand for and Supply of Ph.D. Manpower, 1972-1975," *Monthly Labor Review*, December 1975.)

The following states, in particular, may wish to determine whether their offerings are now excessive:[5]

Alabama	New York
Illinois	North Carolina
Indiana	North Dakota
Louisiana	Ohio
Michigan	South Dakota
Mississippi	Tennessee
Missouri	Texas
New Mexico	Virginia

Strong caution is very much in order at this point. Although there is an impending surplus of Ph.D.'s, there are serious deficiencies in the supply of members of minority groups with Ph.D.'s. There are also deficiencies in the supply of women in some fields. We believe that the drastic cutbacks that have occurred in federal fellowships programs are particularly disastrous in relation to these deficiencies—at a time when the federal government is putting pressure on universities and colleges to hire more minority and women faculty members.

It is also important to recognize that, when we speak of a surplus in the output of Ph.D.'s, we are referring primarily to the fact that too many doctoral-granting institutions were developed during the rapid expansion period of the 1960s. We are not recommending wholesale cutbacks in Ph.D. programs of institutions with long-established and high-quality doctoral programs. Not only is there a tendency for some forecasts to exaggerate the impending overall surplus of Ph.D.'s, but there is also a tendency for some commentators to ignore the fact that the future job market for Ph.D.'s will be much more favorable in some fields than in others.

Health Science Centers. In a report in 1970, the Carnegie Com-

---

[5] Estimated by determining the number of new programs started since 1960 (the number depending on the size of the state) which have drawn very small numbers of students.

mission on Higher Education[6] recommended nine new medical schools, not on grounds that they were needed to meet national requirements for doctors (and other health care personnel) but for the sake of service to a neglected surrounding area. Five schools (two in one area) have been started in these locations. In addition, 13 other new schools have been started or are fully authorized—two of these are in Georgia, two in Ohio, and two in Texas. There is little evidence that the southern states (with the possible exception of Florida) need additional medical schools, yet schools have also been started in North Carolina, South Carolina, Tennessee, and West Virginia (in addition to Georgia and Texas) beyond those found necessary for geographical reasons by the Carnegie Commission. The development in Ohio seems particularly excessive. We believe that the following states, in particular, may have developed or may be developing surplus facilities:[7]

Georgia	Tennessee
North Carolina	Texas
Ohio	West Virginia

A number of new law schools (20 in total) have been started and accredited in recent years.[8] The total number of law school graduates given degrees each year more than doubled in the 1960s. Already, law school graduates are finding difficulty entering practice. However, law schools are less expensive than medical schools to build and to operate, and lawyers can enter many more endeavors that utilize their training than can doctors. Yet a caution is in order.

---

[6]*Higher Education and the Nation's Health: Policies for Medical and Dental Education* (New York: McGraw-Hill, 1970).

[7]Each of these states has developed, or is planning, one or more new medical schools in communities in which no new medical school was recommended by the Carnegie Commission. See the information on medical schools in "Medical Education in the United States, 1974-75," *Journal of the American Medical Association*, 1975, *234* (13), 1333 and 1408-1409.

[8]Thirteen of these are in four states: California, New York, Ohio, and Texas.

Deficits—Essential to Correct

Deficits still exist, despite the surpluses resulting from past developments. This is inevitable in a dynamic situation. It is not inevitable, however, that they will be recognized and corrected within a reasonable period of time. In addition to low levels of provision of student places and of financial support set forth in Sections 4, 5 and 6, we find deficits in four special areas:

Open Access Places. A sufficiency of places now exists, and prospectively will exist at least until the middle 1990s, to take care of all students, except in the one category of open access places. These are defined as places open at low or no tuition to all high school graduates (with necessary skill requirements). They are best supplied by community colleges and by comprehensive colleges with two-year programs comparable to those in community colleges. We believe that the possibility of such deficits should be particularly examined in all large metropolitan areas and in the following states as a whole:[9]

Delaware	New Mexico
Idaho	New York (SUNY)
Indiana	North Dakota
Iowa	Ohio
Kentucky	Oregon
Maine	Pennsylvania
Maryland	Rhode Island
Massachusetts	South Carolina
Minnesota	South Dakota
Mississippi	Utah
Nevada	Vermont
New Hampshire	West Virginia
New Jersey	Wisconsin

(See *Supplement,* A-3 for large metropolitan areas which may, in particular, need more open access places.)

[9]Estimated by looking at tuition levels (above the average for all community colleges of $250 per year), at admission requirements, and at the geographical spread of community colleges and two-year programs in comprehensive colleges.

State Scholarship Programs. The states have made impressive progress in developing student aid programs in recent years. Ten years ago, only about 15 states had such programs, and total expenditures were only $72 million. By 1975-76, total appropriations by the states for comprehensive undergraduate student aid programs amounted to $500 million, and 42 states were providing funds for such programs. Under the stimulus of the federal State Student Incentive Grant (SSIG) program, the number of states providing student aid increased particularly rapidly from 1972 on. By the fall of 1975, all of the states had taken steps to implement student aid programs that would qualify for federal SSIG grants, but seven states (and the District of Columbia) had not appropriated any funds, and Tennessee had discontinued appropriations pending settlement of a challenge to the constitutionality of its program in the courts.

Yet the variations in amounts made available under these programs are exceedingly wide. Only 14 states provided an average of more than $50 per full-time-equivalent student enrolled in higher education in 1975-76, while there were 25 states in which average amounts appropriated were either less than $10 or zero (Figure 14). Our estimates suggest that the cost of a fully funded tuition aid program would be about $200 per full-time-equivalent student, of which the state share would be about $135 (with the funds actually allocated, of course, to low-income students).[10] Only three states—Illinois, New York, and Pennsylvania, provided more than an average of $135 in 1975-76.

We call particular attention to the following states which have not yet begun support of state scholarship programs:

Alabama	New Mexico
Alaska	Tennessee (in abeyance
Arizona	pending court action)
Nevada	Wyoming
New Hampshire	

[10]See the estimates in Carnegie Council on Higher Education, *The Federal Role in Postsecondary Education: Unfinished Business 1975-1980* (San Francisco: Jossey-Bass, 1975), pp. 34-35. The actual amounts would vary from state to state.

Area Health Education Centers. In 1970, the Carnegie Commission recommended the establishment of Area Health Education Centers in 48 of the 50 states.[11] The Health Manpower Act of 1971 made provision for federal assistance in their establishment. In 1975, there were 120 such centers or roughly similar centers providing some of the suggested services (the Commission had recommended 127 but many of them in locations not covered by the 120, and these omitted locations are in 32 states). North Carolina, in particular, has pioneered in this development and with substantial state support.

These centers serve the following functions:

- Advice to local hospitals
- Advice to community agencies in the planning and development of more effective health care delivery systems
- Continuing education for health care personnel, including at the physician level
- Conduct of residency programs (and many doctors undertake practice in the area of their residency)
- Provision of clinical experience for students in M.D., D.D.S., and allied health programs
- Guidance to colleges in developing and improving training programs for the allied health professions

These centers carry with them the prospect of better medical care in many areas where establishment of a health science center, with its medical school, is not warranted. In particular, they encourage doctors to enter into family and primary-care practice in areas now less adequately served.

The following states, in particular, where three or more recommended locations are not yet developed, may wish to examine their progress:[12]

[11]*Higher Education and the Nation's Health: Policies for Medical and Dental Education* (New York: McGraw-Hill, 1970).

[12]Each of these states has at least three fewer area health education centers than were recommended in *Higher Education and the Nation's Health.* Alaska is included, although only two centers were recommended there, because Alaska has no medical school, and thus the need for centers is critical.

Alaska	Mississippi
Arkansas	New Jersey
Georgia	Pennsylvania
Maryland	Texas
Massachusetts	Washington
Michigan	

Health Science Centers. We continue to recommend, for geographical reasons only, new health science centers in Phoenix, Arizona (a large and growing population center); in Delaware (none now exists in the state); and possibly Orlando, Florida (a rapidly growing area).

These deficits are modest in total, but each constitutes an important failure to provide a well-rounded system of state-supported higher education. The removal of these deficits will contribute to greater equality of opportunity for our youth and to better health for all of our people.

Accomplishments of Special Note

The existence of surpluses and deficits should not obscure the fact that much has been done very well. It is more common, in our current age of disillusionment and disenchantment, to concentrate on failures than on successes, but there have been many successful programs in many states. The listings that follow concentrate on the states at the top of our several scales of accomplishment, rather than on those at the bottom.

A number of states have made a particular effort to supply large numbers of places, compared with the size of their populations, for students in public institutions of higher education, and in particular:[13]

Arizona	Oregon
California	Washington

A substantial number of states have made a special effort

---

[13]Figure 18, Section 4.

to place community colleges within commuting distance of all
or nearly all of their people, including:

Arizona	New York[14]
California	North Carolina
Florida	Oklahoma
Hawaii	Oregon
Illinois	Texas
Iowa	Washington

A significant number of states have created public universities (and some colleges) that have drawn, in national competition, substantial federal research funds in total or in relation to
the population of their states:[15]

Alaska	New Mexico
California	Oregon
Colorado	Texas
Hawaii	Utah
Michigan	Washington
Minnesota	Wisconsin

Similarly, a large number of states have public universities
(and colleges) whose graduate faculties have been rated as having elements of distinction, again in total or in relation to the
population of the state.[16]

California	Michigan
Colorado	Minnesota
Illinois	North Carolina
Indiana	Oregon
Iowa	Washington
Kansas	Wisconsin

[14]We cite New York, however, as a deficit state for open access because of
the relatively high tuition at the community colleges within SUNY (not
CUNY).

[15]Figure 21, Section 4.

[16]*Supplement*, Λ-6.

Half a dozen states spend a particularly large proportion of state personal income on public support of higher education:[17]

Alaska	Utah
Arizona	Wisconsin
California	Wyoming

And several states are outstanding in the absolute level of their expenditures per student in public institutions:[18]

Alaska	Wisconsin
New York	

A few states quite early and quite completely converted their teachers colleges into comprehensive colleges and universities. Among them are:[19]

California	Texas
Michigan	

Since 1971, several states have imposed a moratorium, for longer or shorter periods of time, on new doctoral programs:[20]

Florida	New York
Idaho	South Dakota
Louisiana	Washington

One state has done especially well in the creation of Area Health Education Centers:[21]

North Carolina

[17]Figure 22, Section 5.

[18]Figure 23, Section 5.

[19]Selection based on numerous sources relating to the history of state colleges.

[20]Data developed from publications of the Education Commission of the States and other sources.

[21]North Carolina has a particularly comprehensive network of nine AHEC's well distributed throughout the state and is one of the very few

An increasing number of states have developed effective state scholarship programs but particularly:[22]

Illinois	Pennsylvania
New Jersey	Vermont
New York	

Several states, in recent times, have done especially well in increasing the support of their public research university or universities:[23]

Arizona	Massachusetts
Arkansas	Mississippi
Connecticut	New Jersey
Georgia	North Carolina
Hawaii	Texas

A few states have done remarkably well in raising per student support in public institutions, including:[24]

Arkansas	Mississippi
Minnesota	Wisconsin

Several states have prepared reasonably effective state plans for higher education that have had an impact on the development of higher education within their states and that have stood the test of time:[25]

---

states to allocate substantial state funds (augmenting federal funds) for the development of AHEC's.

[22] Figure 14.

[23] Expenditures per weighted FTE students in research universities from state funds increased by 40 percent or more from 1959-60 to 1974-75 in each of these states. These data are not shown for individual states, but are summarized for 35 states combined on the left side of Figure 25 and, for groups of states, in the third column of *Supplement*, A-17.

[24] *Supplement*, A-15.

[25] Based on a special analysis of the Carnegie Council, taking into account (1) the effectiveness of the planning process, (2) the quality of the product, and (3) the degree of impact on the development of the system of higher education.

　　　　　　California　　　　　　New York
　　　　　　Florida　　　　　　　Oklahoma
　　　　　　Illinois　　　　　　　Washington

Several states have made an especially good start toward the support of their private colleges and universities:[26]

　　　　　　Alaska　　　　　　　New York
　　　　　　Illinois　　　　　　　Pennsylvania
　　　　　　Michigan　　　　　　South Carolina
　　　　　　New Jersey

These lists are not complete, but they are indications of many accomplishments of importance in many states.

[26]Figure 29, Section 6.

Figure 14. Appropriations for comprehensive state undergraduate
student aid programs per full-time-equivalent enrolled student,
by state, 1975-76

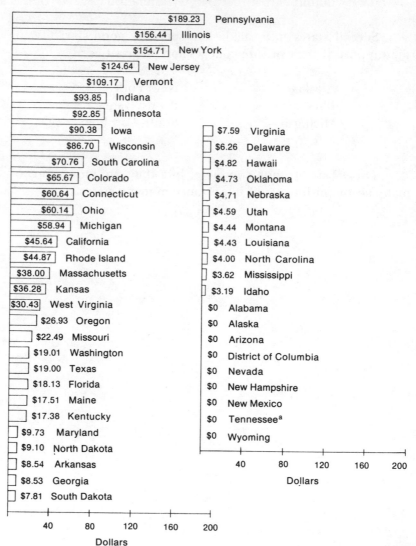

$189.23	Pennsylvania
$156.44	Illinois
$154.71	New York
$124.64	New Jersey
$109.17	Vermont
$93.85	Indiana
$92.85	Minnesota
$90.38	Iowa
$86.70	Wisconsin
$70.76	South Carolina
$65.67	Colorado
$60.64	Connecticut
$60.14	Ohio
$58.94	Michigan
$45.64	California
$44.87	Rhode Island
$38.00	Massachusetts
$36.28	Kansas
$30.43	West Virginia
$26.93	Oregon
$22.49	Missouri
$19.01	Washington
$19.00	Texas
$18.13	Florida
$17.51	Maine
$17.38	Kentucky
$9.73	Maryland
$9.10	North Dakota
$8.54	Arkansas
$8.53	Georgia
$7.81	South Dakota

$7.59	Virginia
$6.26	Delaware
$4.82	Hawaii
$4.73	Oklahoma
$4.71	Nebraska
$4.59	Utah
$4.44	Montana
$4.43	Louisiana
$4.00	North Carolina
$3.62	Mississippi
$3.19	Idaho
$0	Alabama
$0	Alaska
$0	Arizona
$0	District of Columbia
$0	Nevada
$0	New Hampshire
$0	New Mexico
$0	Tennessee[a]
$0	Wyoming

[a]Program is being contested in the courts.

Sources: "State Scholarship Programs," *Chronicle of Higher Education*, November 17, 1975, pp. 6-7; U.S. National Center for Education Statistics, *Opening Fall Enrollment, Fall 1975 (Higher Education) Preliminary Data* (Washington, D.C.: U.S. Government Printing Office, 1975).

4

Diversity
of Structures

Support for institutions of higher education is divided approximately as follows: [1]

- State and local governments—43 percent
- Federal government—25 percent
- Private sources—32 percent

State support for institutions is heavily concentrated on public colleges and universities, although most states now provide some form of subsidy for the private sector as well. Federal support is spread more or less evenly over both public and private institutions, although concentrated somewhat more heavily on private institutions. Private support is comparatively more concentrated on private institutions. Consequently, when one is talking about the states, attention is directed more heavily toward the public sector of higher education than when one is talking about the federal government or about private sources of support.

Public institutions of higher education now constitute 48 percent of all institutions of higher education, provide 78 percent of all currently filled student places, and spend 68 percent of all funds (Figure 15). The states are best viewed, however,

[1] All research funds are included in these data.

not as an entirety, in our tripartite support structure, but rather one at a time. When viewed in detail, each seems to constitute a separate case. It is important to understand this diversity for at least these reasons:

• It is essential to an understanding of higher education in the United States, which is marked by diversity to a greater extent than is almost any other nation of the world. Japan stands closest to the United States in this respect.
• It is helpful in understanding the United States—regional differences, different histories of the separate states, autonomy of the states in making educational policy, rise and fall of state populations, and changes in sources of employment among the states—in short, the great pluralism of American society.
• It explains why it is difficult to generalize about the states and to make recommendations which apply to them all equally—or even to some of them at all.
• It also explains why the federal government could not easily take over higher education and make it into a single national system, as is the case in most other nations; and why, in matters under state control (such as tuition policy),[2] it is hard for the federal government even to exercise much influence.

Patterns. The diversity among the states is substantial:

• Some states have large systems; some small (Figure 16). A few have enrollments comparable to those of entire nations (Figure 17).
• Some provide comparatively many student places, some comparatively few (Figure 18).
• Some rely heavily on private institutions to care for their enrollment, one not at all (Figure 19).
• Some, in their public sector, have comparatively heavy enroll-

---

[2]Carnegie Council on Higher Education, *Low or No Tuition: The Feasibility of a National Policy for the First Two Years of College* (San Francisco: Jossey-Bass, 1975).

ments in their universities, some in their comprehensive colleges and universities, and some in their community colleges (Figure 20).
· Some rely heavily on their public institutions and others on their private institutions for their highest-quality research efforts and graduate training (Figure 21, and *Supplement,* A-4 through A-8).

Observations. While each state has its own individual set of defining characteristics, some, more generalized observations can be made:

· The states with the highest ratio of enrollments to population (leaving aside the District of Columbia, which is a very special case of a single city) are in the West (Arizona, California, Oregon, Utah, and Washington) and in the Northeast, where strong private segments attract students on a nationwide basis (Connecticut, Massachusetts, New York, Rhode Island, and Vermont). Six of the seven lowest states are in the South; the seventh is Alaska.
· Among types of public institutions, it is generally the least-populous states that rely the most heavily on their universities to carry the larger share of enrollments. They tend to have few institutions and consequently to make them more all-purpose. The southern states tend to concentrate their enrollments most heavily in comprehensive colleges and universities, and the western (and some southern) states, in community colleges.
· Only one state (Massachusetts) has a majority of its enrollments in private institutions, and only five others have private enrollments at the 40 percent level or above (New Hampshire, New York, Pennsylvania, Rhode Island, and Vermont). All of these states are in the Northeast. All of the 11 states with 10 percent or less of enrollments in private institutions are located west of the Mississippi.
· A few states rank much higher in federal research and development dollars going to public institutions than they do in the population of the state. This is particularly true in:

Alaska   Oregon
Colorado   Utah
Hawaii   Washington
New Mexico   Wisconsin

This is often a commentary on the quality of their state institutions at the highest academic level, but on other things as well, such as unique locations like Alaska for arctic studies, Hawaii for tropical studies, and Colorado for high-altitude research; such as the comparative reliance of the state on public, compared with private, research universities (all of these states rely heavily on their public research universities); and such as the presence of a medical school with substantial federal funding in a state with a small population.

· States that rank low are:

Connecticut   Missouri
Louisiana   New Jersey
Maine   South Carolina
Massachusetts

Four of these states are in the Northeast (and three of them have very strong private institutions), and three are in southern or border states. As the southern states become wealthier economically, it may be expected that they will spend more on their research universities and that these universities, in turn, will draw more federal research support by the quality of their faculties.

· In 11 states, more than half of the federal research and development funds received in higher education goes to private institutions. Eight of them are in the Northeast. The other three are Illinois, Missouri, and Tennessee. Each of these states has one or more academically strong private research universities (*Supplement*, A-4).

As is to be expected, the states doing best in relation to their population rank in receipt of federal research and development funds are those with distinctive locations or with strong public or strong private research universities. Alaska

illustrates the first category, Washington the second, and Connecticut the third (*Supplement*, A-5).

- The states with the greatest strength in their public university graduate faculties are California and Michigan. California and New York rank first based on all institutions, but a number of smaller states do exceptionally well compared to their population size. Generally the greatest academic strength at the graduate level is concentrated in the Northeast, the Middle West, and the West Coast (*Supplement*, A-6, A-7, and A-8).

- Overall, public institutions receive about 58 percent of all federal research and development funds (private, 42 percent) and have about 47 percent of all departmental graduate faculties rated as "distinguished" (private, 53 percent). Thus distinction at the level of attracting federal research funds and of graduate training is roughly 50-50 between public and private institutions throughout the nation, but with enormous variations from state to state.

The one simple statement about the states and higher education that is true is that no simple statement about them is true.

Figure 15. Higher education in its totality—number of institutions, size of enrollments, and total of current-funds expenditures, by state and local, private, and federal sectors

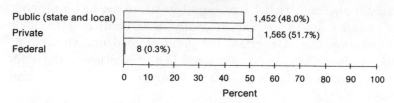

Number of institutions, 1974-75

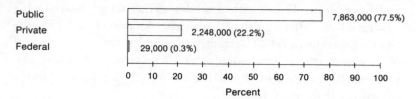

Total enrollments, 1974-75

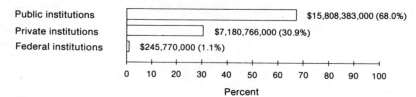

Current funds expenditures, 1973-74

Note: See *Supplement,* A-9 for state-by-state data.

Figure 16. States ranked by total enrollment in higher education, 1974, with numbers of institutions by control of institution

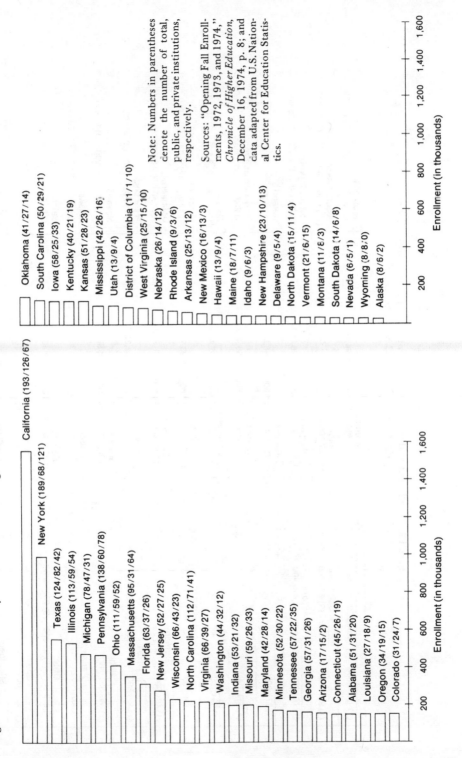

California (193/126/67)

New York (189/68/121)

Texas (124/82/42)

Illinois (113/59/54)

Michigan (78/47/31)

Pennsylvania (138/60/78)

Ohio (111/59/52)

Massachusetts (95/31/64)

Florida (63/37/26)

New Jersey (52/27/25)

Wisconsin (66/43/23)

North Carolina (112/71/41)

Virginia (66/39/27)

Washington (44/32/12)

Indiana (53/21/32)

Missouri (59/26/33)

Maryland (42/28/14)

Minnesota (52/30/22)

Tennessee (57/22/35)

Georgia (57/31/26)

Arizona (17/15/2)

Connecticut (45/26/19)

Alabama (51/31/20)

Louisiana (27/18/9)

Oregon (34/19/15)

Colorado (31/24/7)

Enrollment (in thousands)
200 400 600 800 1,000 1,200 1,400 1,600

Oklahoma (41/27/14)

South Carolina (50/29/21)

Iowa (58/25/33)

Kentucky (40/21/19)

Kansas (51/28/23)

Mississippi (42/26/16)

Utah (13/9/4)

District of Columbia (11/1/10)

West Virginia (25/15/10)

Nebraska (26/14/12)

Rhode Island (9/3/6)

Arkansas (25/13/12)

New Mexico (16/13/3)

Hawaii (13/9/4)

Maine (18/7/11)

Idaho (9/6/3)

New Hampshire (23/10/13)

Delaware (9/5/4)

North Dakota (15/11/4)

Vermont (21/6/15)

Montana (11/8/3)

South Dakota (14/6/8)

Nevada (6/5/1)

Wyoming (8/8/0)

Alaska (8/6/2)

Enrollment (in thousands)
200 400 600 800 1,000 1,200 1,400 1,600

Note: Numbers in parentheses denote the number of total, public, and private institutions, respectively.

Sources: "Opening Fall Enrollments, 1972, 1973, and 1974," *Chronicle of Higher Education*, December 16, 1974, p. 8; and data adapted from U.S. National Center for Education Statistics.

Figure 17. Enrollment of degree-credit students in institutions of higher education in OECD countries and U.S. states, 1970[a]

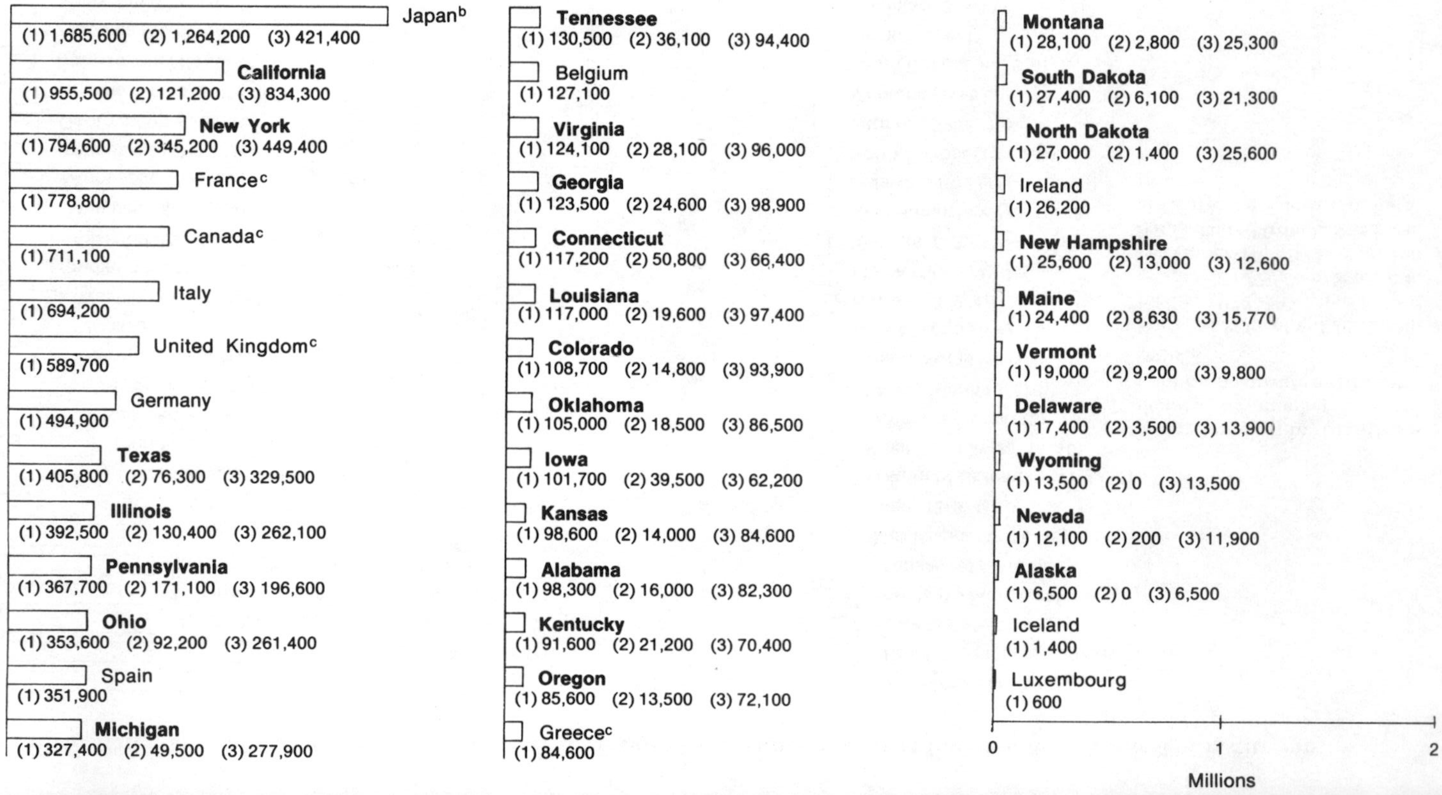

Japan[b]
(1) 1,685,600 (2) 1,264,200 (3) 421,400

California
(1) 955,500 (2) 121,200 (3) 834,300

New York
(1) 794,600 (2) 345,200 (3) 449,400

France[c]
(1) 778,800

Canada[c]
(1) 711,100

Italy
(1) 694,200

United Kingdom[c]
(1) 589,700

Germany
(1) 494,900

Texas
(1) 405,800 (2) 76,300 (3) 329,500

Illinois
(1) 392,500 (2) 130,400 (3) 262,100

Pennsylvania
(1) 367,700 (2) 171,100 (3) 196,600

Ohio
(1) 353,600 (2) 92,200 (3) 261,400

Spain
(1) 351,900

Michigan
(1) 327,400 (2) 49,500 (3) 277,900

Tennessee
(1) 130,500 (2) 36,100 (3) 94,400

Belgium
(1) 127,100

Virginia
(1) 124,100 (2) 28,100 (3) 96,000

Georgia
(1) 123,500 (2) 24,600 (3) 98,900

Connecticut
(1) 117,200 (2) 50,800 (3) 66,400

Louisiana
(1) 117,000 (2) 19,600 (3) 97,400

Colorado
(1) 108,700 (2) 14,800 (3) 93,900

Oklahoma
(1) 105,000 (2) 18,500 (3) 86,500

Iowa
(1) 101,700 (2) 39,500 (3) 62,200

Kansas
(1) 98,600 (2) 14,000 (3) 84,600

Alabama
(1) 98,300 (2) 16,000 (3) 82,300

Kentucky
(1) 91,600 (2) 21,200 (3) 70,400

Oregon
(1) 85,600 (2) 13,500 (3) 72,100

Greece[c]
(1) 84,600

Montana
(1) 28,100 (2) 2,800 (3) 25,300

South Dakota
(1) 27,400 (2) 6,100 (3) 21,300

North Dakota
(1) 27,000 (2) 1,400 (3) 25,600

Ireland
(1) 26,200

New Hampshire
(1) 25,600 (2) 13,000 (3) 12,600

Maine
(1) 24,400 (2) 8,630 (3) 15,770

Vermont
(1) 19,000 (2) 9,200 (3) 9,800

Delaware
(1) 17,400 (2) 3,500 (3) 13,900

Wyoming
(1) 13,500 (2) 0 (3) 13,500

Nevada
(1) 12,100 (2) 200 (3) 11,900

Alaska
(1) 6,500 (2) 0 (3) 6,500

Iceland
(1) 1,400

Luxembourg
(1) 600

0   1   2
Millions

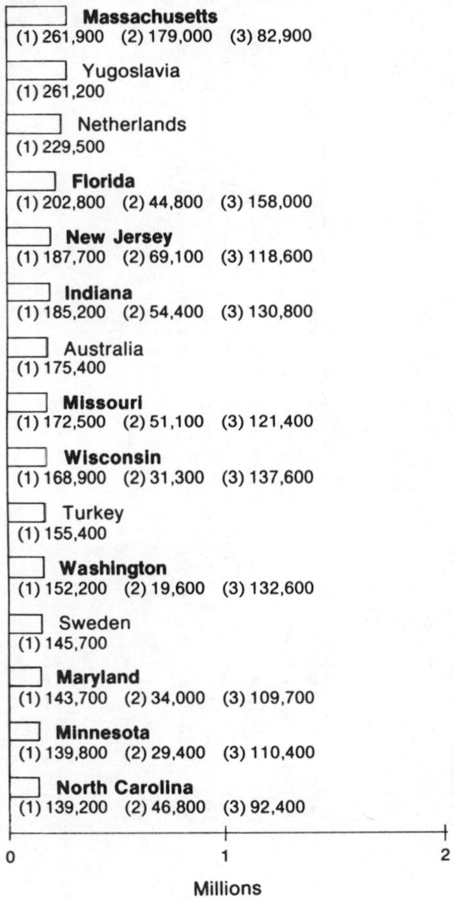

Massachusetts
(1) 261,900 (2) 179,000 (3) 82,900
Yugoslavia
(1) 261,200
Netherlands
(1) 229,500
Florida
(1) 202,800 (2) 44,800 (3) 158,000
New Jersey
(1) 187,700 (2) 69,100 (3) 118,600
Indiana
(1) 185,200 (2) 54,400 (3) 130,800
Australia
(1) 175,400
Missouri
(1) 172,500 (2) 51,100 (3) 121,400
Wisconsin
(1) 168,900 (2) 31,300 (3) 137,600
Turkey
(1) 155,400
Washington
(1) 152,200 (2) 19,600 (3) 132,600
Sweden
(1) 145,700
Maryland
(1) 143,700 (2) 34,000 (3) 109,700
Minnesota
(1) 139,800 (2) 29,400 (3) 110,400
North Carolina
(1) 139,200 (2) 46,800 (3) 92,400
0
1
2
Millions

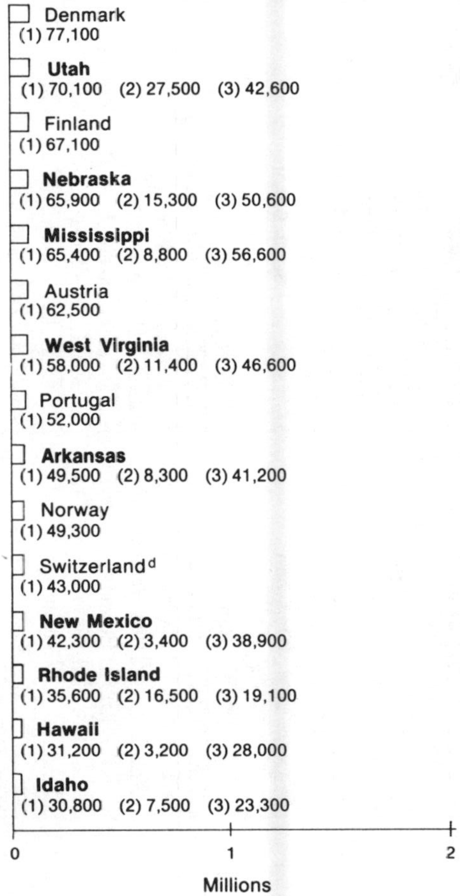

Denmark
(1) 77,100
Utah
(1) 70,100 (2) 27,500 (3) 42,600
Finland
(1) 67,100
Nebraska
(1) 65,900 (2) 15,300 (3) 50,600
Mississippi
(1) 65,400 (2) 8,800 (3) 56,600
Austria
(1) 62,500
West Virginia
(1) 58,000 (2) 11,400 (3) 46,600
Portugal
(1) 52,000
Arkansas
(1) 49,500 (2) 8,300 (3) 41,200
Norway
(1) 49,300
Switzerland[d]
(1) 43,000
New Mexico
(1) 42,300 (2) 3,400 (3) 38,900
Rhode Island
(1) 35,600 (2) 16,500 (3) 19,100
Hawaii
(1) 31,200 (2) 3,200 (3) 28,000
Idaho
(1) 30,800 (2) 7,500 (3) 23,300
0
1
2
Millions

Note: Bars show jurisdictions ranked by total enrollment; numbers under bars indicate (1) total enrollment, (2) private enrollment, and (3) public enrollment.

[a]Data for OECD countries other than the United States are reasonably comparable with U.S. data. They include enrollments in university or university-type education, which is defined as long education, lasting three or four years at least, for which a secondary school leaving certificate is required and which leads to a first degree that may, in turn, lead on to higher diplomas. Nonuniversity education is also included and is defined as relatively short education for which a secondary school leaving certificate is not always required and which leads to a diploma regarded as below first degree level.

[b]Public and private enrollment in 1970 were estimated from 1967 data.

[c]Data are for 1969.

[d]Data are for 1968.

Sources: Data for countries other than the United States are from the Organisation for Economic Co-operation and Development, *Towards Mass Higher Education: Issues and Dilemmas* (Paris, 1974).

Figure 18. Ratio of total enrollment in higher education to population
aged 18 to 24, by state and control of institution, 1974-75

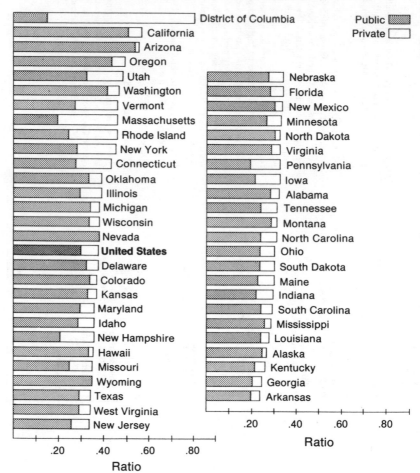

Note: See *Supplement*, A-10 for undergraduate degree-credit enrollment of persons
aged 18 to 24 as a percentage of their age group.

Sources: "Opening Fall Enrollments, 1972, 1973, and 1974," *Chronicle of Higher
Education*, December 16, 1974, p. 8; U.S. Bureau of the Census, "Projections of the
Population of Voting Age, for States: November 1974," *Current Population Reports*,
Series P-25, No. 526 (Washington, D.C.: U.S. Government Printing Office, 1974).

Figure 19. Enrollment in private institutions as a percentage of total enrollment in higher education, by state, 1974

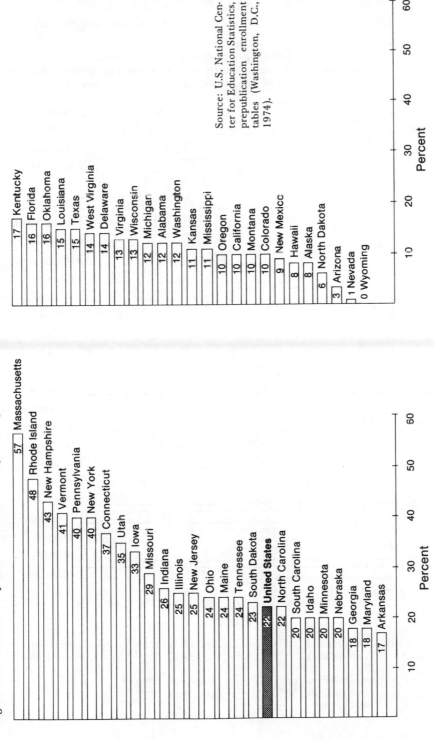

Source: U.S. National Center for Education Statistics, prepublication enrollment tables (Washington, D.C., 1974).

Figure 20. Distribution of enrollment in public institutions of higher
education in each state, by type of institution, with states ranked by
percentage of public enrollment in universities, 1974

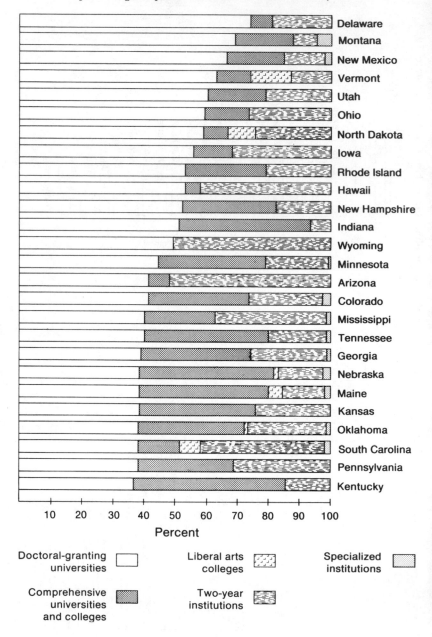

Figure 20 *(continued)*

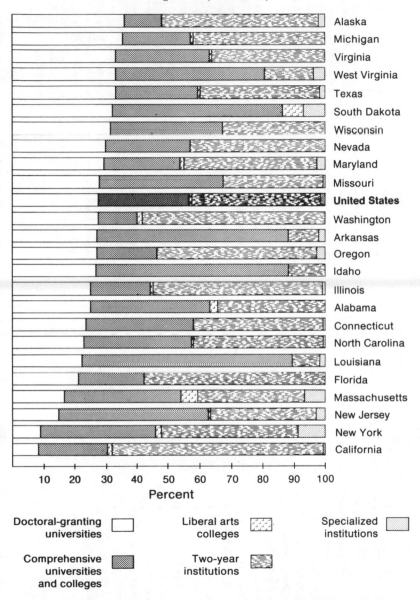

Doctoral-granting universities

Comprehensive universities and colleges

Liberal arts colleges

Two-year institutions

Specialized institutions

Note: For distribution of full-time-equivalent enrollment in public institutions, see *Supplement,* A-11.

Source: Adapted from U.S. National Center for Education Statistics data.

Figure 21. Federal funds for research and development, fiscal year 1974, to public institutions, compared with population rank of states

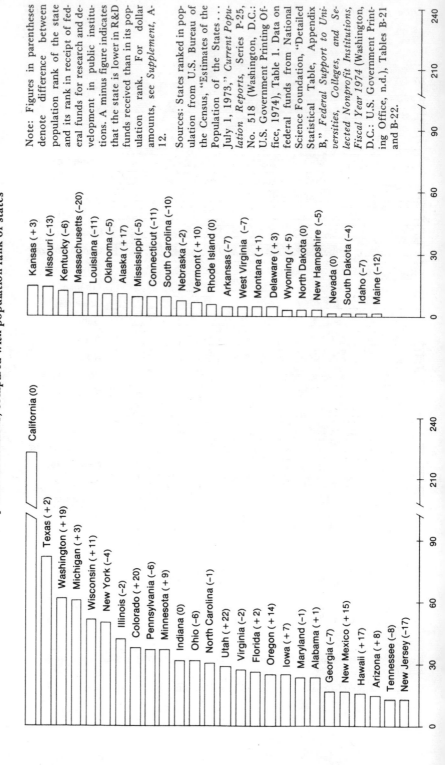

California (0)

Texas (+2)

Washington (+19)
Michigan (+3)
Wisconsin (+11)
New York (−4)
Illinois (−2)
Colorado (+20)
Pennsylvania (−6)
Minnesota (+9)
Indiana (0)
Ohio (−6)
North Carolina (−1)
Utah (+22)
Virginia (−2)
Florida (+2)
Oregon (+14)
Iowa (+7)
Maryland (−1)
Alabama (+1)
Georgia (−7)
New Mexico (+15)
Hawaii (+17)
Arizona (+8)
Tennessee (−8)
New Jersey (−17)

Kansas (+3)
Missouri (−13)
Kentucky (−6)
Massachusetts (−20)
Louisiana (−11)
Oklahoma (−5)
Alaska (+17)
Mississippi (−5)
Connecticut (−11)
South Carolina (−10)
Nebraska (−2)
Vermont (+10)
Rhode Island (0)
Arkansas (−7)
West Virginia (−7)
Montana (+1)
Delaware (+3)
Wyoming (+5)
North Dakota (0)
New Hampshire (−5)
Nevada (0)
South Dakota (−4)
Idaho (−7)
Maine (−12)

Note: Figures in parentheses denote difference between population rank of the state and its rank in receipt of federal funds for research and development in public institutions. A minus figure indicates that the state is lower in R&D funds received than in its population rank. For dollar amounts, see *Supplement*, A-12.

Sources: States ranked in population from U.S. Bureau of the Census, "Estimates of the Population of the States . . . July 1, 1973," *Current Population Reports*, Series P-25, No. 518 (Washington, D.C.: U.S. Government Printing Office, 1974), Table 1. Data on federal funds from National Science Foundation, "Detailed Statistical Table, Appendix B," *Federal Support to Universities, Colleges, and Selected Nonprofit Institutions, Fiscal Year 1974* (Washington, D.C.: U.S. Government Printing Office, n.d.), Tables B-21 and B-22.

5

Diversity
of Support

State support for higher education follows no conforming patterns from state to state. Variations are the dominant theme.

Effort. The percentage of state personal income spent by state and local governments on higher education is a good indication of the taxpayer "effort" of each state. On this basis, some states, particularly Arizona, Wisconsin, and Wyoming, make over two and one-half times the effort of other states, particularly Massachusetts, New Hampshire, and Ohio (Figure 22). Generally, the highest-effort states are in the West, where there are fewer enrollments in private institutions (Wyoming has none), and lowest in the East, where private enrollments are more substantial. But there are many exceptions to this rule. Utah makes a substantial public effort even though it has substantial private enrollments; so does New York. Nevada, Oklahoma and South Dakota, on the other hand, make a comparatively small public effort even though they have relatively few private enrollments.

Concern. Expenditures per FTE student in public institutions may be said to reflect "concern." These expenditures may be relatively high if the state has high levels of per capita income and/or if public enrollments are low compared to population,

even though "effort" is low. Thus the District of Columbia, with low "effort," still evidences high "concern." Expenditures in the highest state, Alaska, regardless of reasons, are almost four times higher than in the lowest state, Oklahoma (Figure 23). Among the more populous states, New York ranks highest and Ohio lowest.

Competitive position of higher education. The "competitive position" of higher education as against other types of expenditures by the states is a third way of looking at comparative support. The average of state appropriations spent on higher education is about 15 percent of revenues, but the range is enormous: from over 36 percent in South Dakota to about 8 percent in Massachusetts and Rhode Island—a ratio of over 4 to 1 (Figure 24). Generally, the less-populous states with high percentages of public enrollments are at the top of the list; but the states at the bottom of the list have few, if any, common characteristics.

Viewed in these three different ways, the states line up frequently in quite odd patterns. Oklahoma, for example, is low in "effort," the lowest of all in "concern," but among the highest in "competitive position." Alaska, by contrast, is high on the first measure (effort), highest on the second (concern), and among the lowest on the third (competitive position). Overall, Wisconsin and Wyoming have the highest ratings, and New Hampshire the lowest.

Some spectacular changes have taken place in all three of these measures over recent years:

- Some states, particularly Alaska, New York, North Carolina, and Wisconsin, greatly increased their "effort" between 1967-68 and 1973-74; others, including Hawaii, Louisiana, North Dakota, and South Dakota, greatly reduced theirs (*Supplement,* A-14).
- Some states improved upon their "concern," especially Arkansas, Minnesota, Mississippi, and Wisconsin; while others lowered theirs, including Louisiana, Nevada, South Dakota and Vermont (*Supplement,* A-15). A "normal" change over a six-year period, based on historical practice going back to

1930, would have been a rise of 12 to 15 percent—2 to 2.5 percent per year over and above the rise in the cost of living.[1] Only Indiana and Wyoming were within this "normal" range.

• Some states increased the "competitive position" of higher education—Nebraska most notably; and others reduced it— North Dakota and Montana most drastically (*Supplement,* A-16). The latter two, along with South Dakota (noted twice just above) are states that have lost enrollments.

Comparative treatment of public research universities. Generally, the position of public research universities, as a further change, has deteriorated within the totality of state-supported higher education; and, within this category, Research Universities II more than Research Universities I[2] over the 15 years from 1959-60 to 1974-75 (Figure 25). This was a period when former teachers colleges were becoming comprehensive colleges and universities and adding business and engineering programs, among others, and when community colleges were not only spreading rapidly but introducing more technical programs. Both of these developments might be expected to raise costs per student in these types of institutions on a comparative basis; and some of these other institutions started from a very low base of support. On the other hand, costs at research universities would be expected to rise relatively rapidly because of the expansion of very costly Ph.D. and medical-training programs.

---

[1] Carnegie Commission on Higher Education, *The More Effective Use of Resources: An Imperative for Higher Education* (New York: McGraw-Hill, 1972).

[2] In general, The Carnegie Commission on Higher Education classified institutions as Research Universities I if they were among 50 leading universities in terms of federal financial support of academic science in at least two of the academic years between 1968 and 1971, provided they awarded at least 50 Ph.D.'s. Research Universities II were on the list of the 100 leading institutions in terms of federal financial support in at least two of the academic years between 1968 and 1971 and awarded at least 50 Ph.D.'s, or were among the leading 50 institutions in terms of the total number of Ph.D.'s awarded between 1960 and 1970. For further information on the classifications see Carnegie Commission on Higher Education, *A Classification of Institutions of Higher Education* (Berkeley, Calif., 1973).

Regardless of short-run considerations, however, the relative
decline in state expenditures per FTE student in research universities is a source of concern for the long run, even though
federal research and development funds have greatly expanded.
These universities, among the public institutions, are the major
sources for the training of persons at the highest levels of professional skill and for research. Federal funds, while helpful, are
mostly for research and training only in specific fields. States
that have reduced their comparative expenditures the most cluster in the Middle States, including Kansas, Kentucky, Michigan,
Missouri, Tennessee, and Wisconsin. Those that have increased
expenditures on this basis are disproportionately in the South,
including Arkansas, Georgia, Maryland, and Mississippi.

Tuition policies. The states not only determine their own direct
support of higher education, but they also either determine, or
at least influence, the tuition charged to students. Here, patterns vary from the high of Vermont to the low of California in
a range of 7.5 to 1 (Figure 26). Generally, higher tuition is
charged in states with comparatively high private enrollments
and lower tuition where private enrollments are low, although
Massachusetts, with the highest private enrollment, has relatively low public tuition. Public tuition as a percentage of state
expenditures also varies substantially (*Supplement,* A-19). One
state, Vermont, is virtually on a 1 to 1 basis; another, New
Hampshire, is 4 on public expenditures to 3 on tuition; and still
another, Ohio, is 3 to 2. At the other extreme, California is 10
to 1, and others, including Alaska, Arizona, Hawaii, CUNY in
New York, North Carolina, and Texas, are 5 or more to 1. Most
states, however, are in the range of 4 to 1 or 3 to 1.

The income per student received by public institutions of
higher education for instructional and general purposes depends
on a combination of state and local expenditures along with tuition. States can be grouped by their policies on expenditures
and tuition combined (*Supplement,* A-20). As is to be expected,
states with high public expenditures and high tuition spend the
most per student in total, and those with low expenditures and
low tuition spend the least.

There are other explanations for high and low expenditures per student beyond those given above. In particular, they are (a) the faculty/student ratio and (b) the level of faculty salaries in each state. Regardless of anything else, taken together these two factors explain about one-quarter or one-third of the variations (*Supplement,* A-21). Behind these two factors, of course, lie many influencing and determining conditions.

Each state seems to listen to its own drummer or drummers—for some states appear to march in several directions at once.

Figure 22. State expenditures[a] for higher education as a percentage of state personal income, 1973-74

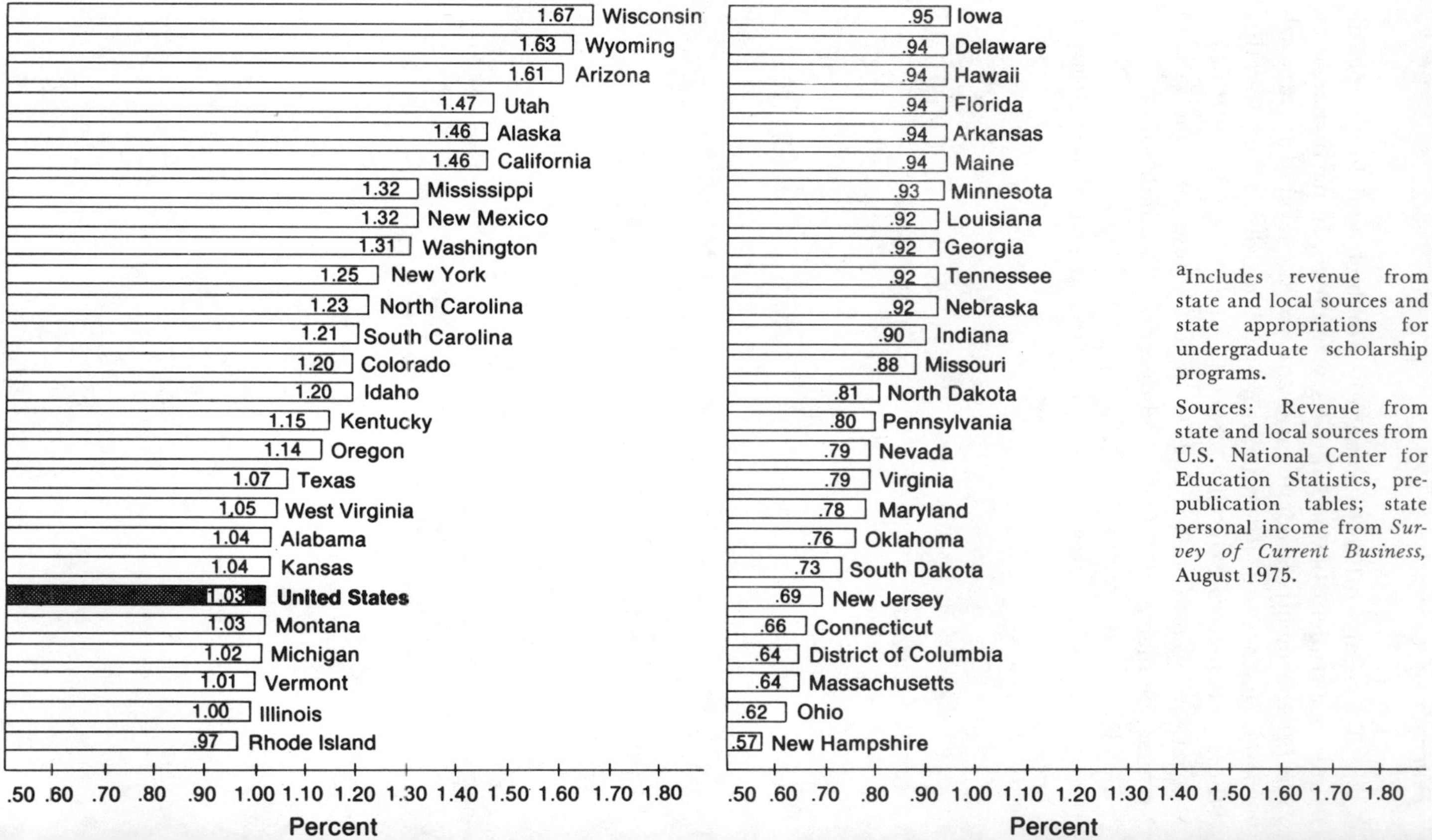
1.67 Wisconsin
1.63 Wyoming
1.61 Arizona
1.47 Utah
1.46 Alaska
1.46 California
1.32 Mississippi
1.32 New Mexico
1.31 Washington
1.25 New York
1.23 North Carolina
1.21 South Carolina
1.20 Colorado
1.20 Idaho
1.15 Kentucky
1.14 Oregon
1.07 Texas
1.05 West Virginia
1.04 Alabama
1.04 Kansas
1.03 United States
1.03 Montana
1.02 Michigan
1.01 Vermont
1.00 Illinois
.97 Rhode Island
.95 Iowa
.94 Delaware
.94 Hawaii
.94 Florida
.94 Arkansas
.94 Maine
.93 Minnesota
.92 Louisiana
.92 Georgia
.92 Tennessee
.92 Nebraska
.90 Indiana
.88 Missouri
.81 North Dakota
.80 Pennsylvania
.79 Nevada
.79 Virginia
.78 Maryland
.76 Oklahoma
.73 South Dakota
.69 New Jersey
.66 Connecticut
.64 District of Columbia
.64 Massachusetts
.62 Ohio
.57 New Hampshire
.50 .60 .70 .80 .90 1.00 1.10 1.20 1.30 1.40 1.50 1.60 1.70 1.80
Percent
.50 .60 .70 .80 .90 1.00 1.10 1.20 1.30 1.40 1.50 1.60 1.70 1.80
Percent

[a]Includes revenue from state and local sources and state appropriations for undergraduate scholarship programs.

Sources: Revenue from state and local sources from U.S. National Center for Education Statistics, prepublication tables; state personal income from *Survey of Current Business*, August 1975.

Figure 23. Expenditures per full-time-equivalent student from state and local sources in public institutions of higher education, 1973-74[a]

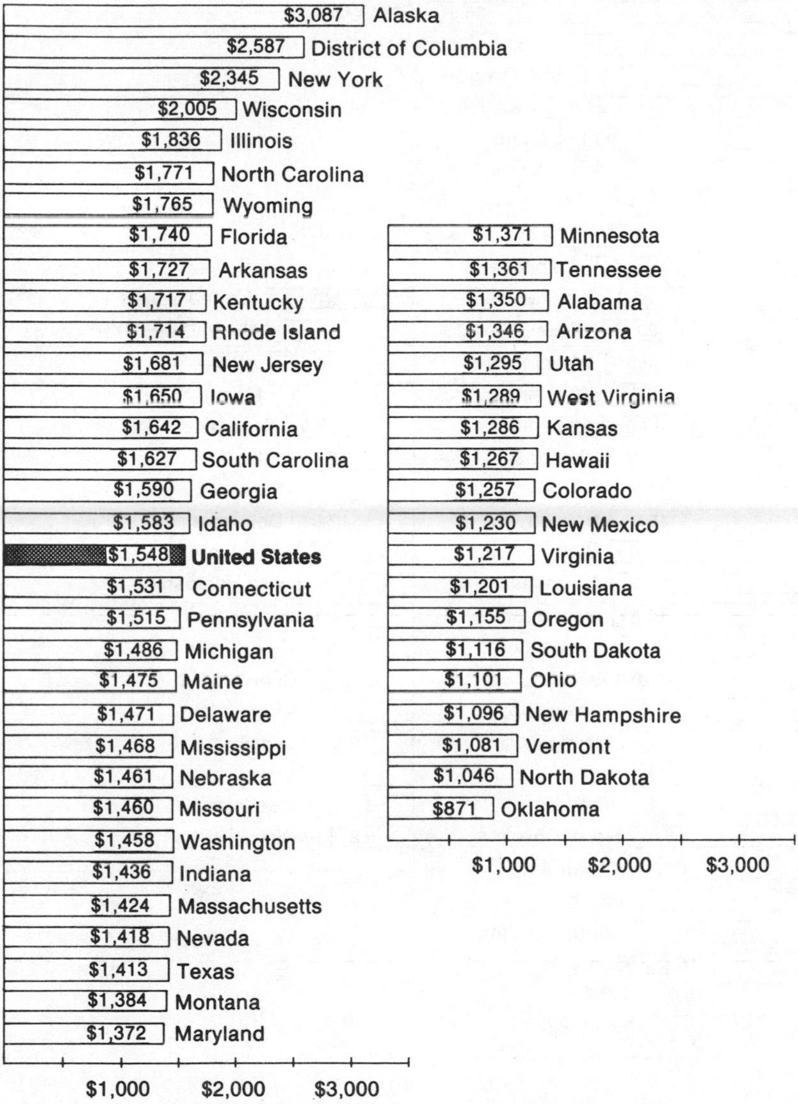

$3,087 Alaska	
$2,587 District of Columbia	
$2,345 New York	
$2,005 Wisconsin	
$1,836 Illinois	
$1,771 North Carolina	
$1,765 Wyoming	
$1,740 Florida	$1,371 Minnesota
$1,727 Arkansas	$1,361 Tennessee
$1,717 Kentucky	$1,350 Alabama
$1,714 Rhode Island	$1,346 Arizona
$1,681 New Jersey	$1,295 Utah
$1,650 Iowa	$1,289 West Virginia
$1,642 California	$1,286 Kansas
$1,627 South Carolina	$1,267 Hawaii
$1,590 Georgia	$1,257 Colorado
$1,583 Idaho	$1,230 New Mexico
$1,548 United States	$1,217 Virginia
$1,531 Connecticut	$1,201 Louisiana
$1,515 Pennsylvania	$1,155 Oregon
$1,486 Michigan	$1,116 South Dakota
$1,475 Maine	$1,101 Ohio
$1,471 Delaware	$1,096 New Hampshire
$1,468 Mississippi	$1,081 Vermont
$1,461 Nebraska	$1,046 North Dakota
$1,460 Missouri	$871 Oklahoma
$1,458 Washington	
$1,436 Indiana	$1,000 $2,000 $3,000
$1,424 Massachusetts	
$1,418 Nevada	
$1,413 Texas	
$1,384 Montana	
$1,372 Maryland	

$1,000 $2,000 $3,000

[a]Postbaccalaureate students in universities are weighted 3 to 1 and postbaccalaureate students in four-year colleges are weighted 2 to 1, in comparison with undergraduates, in computing FTE enrollment.

Source: Adapted from U.S. National Center for Education Statistics data.

Figure 24. State appropriations for higher education as a percentage
of state general revenue, 1974-75

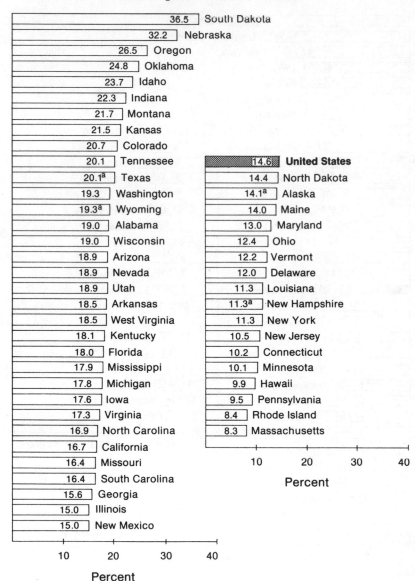

36.5 South Dakota	
32.2 Nebraska	
26.5 Oregon	
24.8 Oklahoma	
23.7 Idaho	
22.3 Indiana	
21.7 Montana	
21.5 Kansas	
20.7 Colorado	
20.1 Tennessee	14.6 United States
20.1[a] Texas	14.4 North Dakota
19.3 Washington	14.1[a] Alaska
19.3[a] Wyoming	14.0 Maine
19.0 Alabama	13.0 Maryland
19.0 Wisconsin	12.4 Ohio
18.9 Arizona	12.2 Vermont
18.9 Nevada	12.0 Delaware
18.9 Utah	11.3 Louisiana
18.5 Arkansas	11.3[a] New Hampshire
18.5 West Virginia	11.3 New York
18.1 Kentucky	10.5 New Jersey
18.0 Florida	10.2 Connecticut
17.9 Mississippi	10.1 Minnesota
17.8 Michigan	9.9 Hawaii
17.6 Iowa	9.5 Pennsylvania
17.3 Virginia	8.4 Rhode Island
16.9 North Carolina	8.3 Massachusetts
16.7 California	
16.4 Missouri	
16.4 South Carolina	
15.6 Georgia	
15.0 Illinois	
15.0 New Mexico	

Percent

[a]Estimated from U.S. National Center for Education Statistics and U.S. Bureau of
the Census data.

Source: Data provided by Lyman Glenny and associates, Center for Research and
Development in Higher Education, University of California, Berkeley, except for
Texas, Wyoming, Alaska, and New Hampshire.

Figure 25. Percentage changes in expenditures per full-time-equivalent student[a] from state and local funds—public research university campuses compared with all other public institutions, 1959-60 to 1974-75 (in constant 1967 dollars)

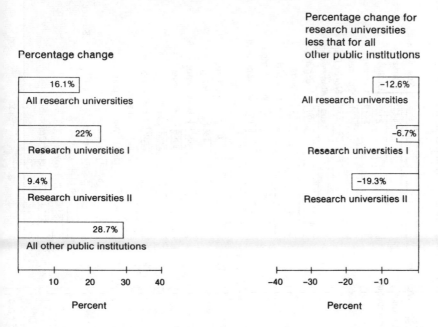

Note: These percentages varied widely from state to state. When states are arranged in groups of six, ranging from Group I, with the least favorable experience for research universities to Group VI, with the most favorable experience for research universities, the groups include the following states:

Group I: Kansas, Kentucky, Michigan, Tennessee, West Virginia, and Wisconsin.
Group II: Colorado, Florida, Missouri, New Jersey, North Carolina, and Washington.
Group III: Alabama, California, Indiana, Minnesota, Ohio, and Oregon.
Group IV: Illinois, Louisiana, Nebraska, Oklahoma, Texas, and Virginia.
Group V: Arizona, Arkansas, Massachusetts, Mississippi, Pennsylvania, and Utah.
Group VI: Connecticut, Georgia, Hawaii, Iowa, and Maryland (only 5 states).

[a]In computing expenditures per FTE, postbaccalaureate students are weighted, as explained in *Supplement,* A-17, footnote *a.*

Source: *Supplement,* A-17.

Figure 26. Average tuition and required fees in public institutions of higher education, by state, 1973-74

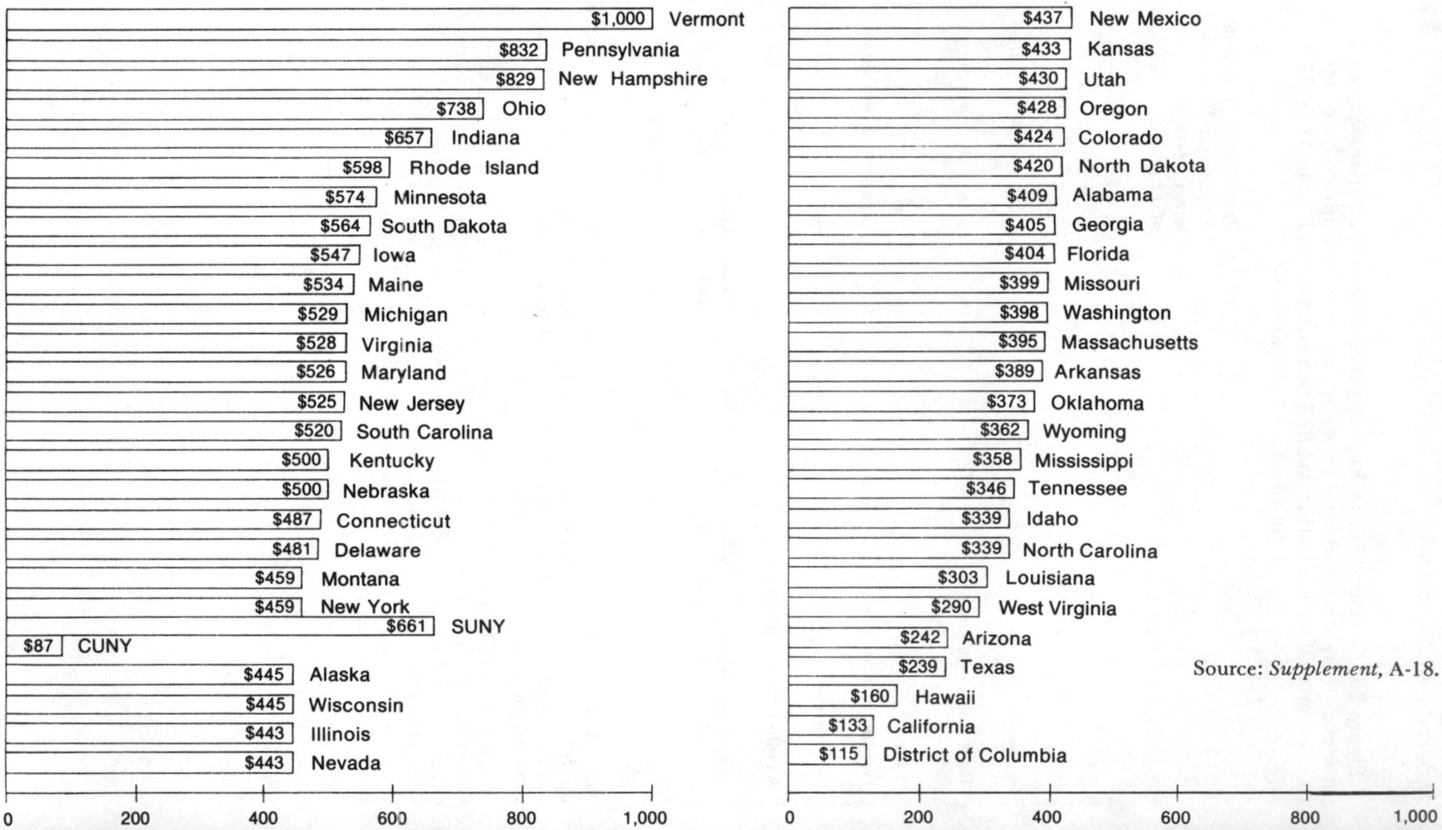

Vermont	$1,000
Pennsylvania	$832
New Hampshire	$829
Ohio	$738
Indiana	$657
Rhode Island	$598
Minnesota	$574
South Dakota	$564
Iowa	$547
Maine	$534
Michigan	$529
Virginia	$528
Maryland	$526
New Jersey	$525
South Carolina	$520
Kentucky	$500
Nebraska	$500
Connecticut	$487
Delaware	$481
Montana	$459
New York	$459
SUNY	$661
CUNY	$87
Alaska	$445
Wisconsin	$445
Illinois	$443
Nevada	$443
New Mexico	$437
Kansas	$433
Utah	$430
Oregon	$428
Colorado	$424
North Dakota	$420
Alabama	$409
Georgia	$405
Florida	$404
Missouri	$399
Washington	$398
Massachusetts	$395
Arkansas	$389
Oklahoma	$373
Wyoming	$362
Mississippi	$358
Tennessee	$346
Idaho	$339
North Carolina	$339
Louisiana	$303
West Virginia	$290
Arizona	$242
Texas	$239
Hawaii	$160
California	$133
District of Columbia	$115

Source: *Supplement*, A-18.

6

Diversity of Relations to the Private Sector

The private sector is an essential part of higher education in the United States:

- It provides 22 percent of all student places.
- It includes 52 percent of all institutions.
- It spends 31 percent of all funds spent by colleges and universities for educational programs.
- It receives 42 percent of all federal research and development funds.
- It has 53 percent of all graduate departments with "distinguished" faculties, and 63 percent of the members of the National Academy of Sciences located in institutions of higher education. Of all Guggenheim fellowships (1964-1975) given to persons in institutions of higher education, 53 percent went to persons in private institutions (*Supplement*, A-13, A-22 and A-23).
- It supplies much of the diversity among all institutions of higher education (Figure 27).

The private sector is also a declining proportion of higher education (Figure 28). This decline in proportion is not due to a reduction of absolute numbers, which have quadrupled since 1929-30, but is, rather, the consequence of the great rise in

public enrollments. However, about one-quarter of private institutions have recently been found to be in "serious" fiscal distress[1] and the tuition gap between public and private institutions is substantial. Usually, public tuition is about one-quarter of private tuition, with the dollar gap for universities and highly selective liberal arts colleges being about $2,100 and for comprehensive institutions and less-selective colleges about $1,400. Public tuition as a percent of private tuition for universities and highly selective colleges is lowest in Louisiana and highest in Utah, and for comprehensive institutions and less-selective colleges is lowest in California and highest in Arkansas and Pennsylvania (*Supplement,* A-25).

In any event, more and more states are now giving aid in one form or another to private institutions (*Supplement,* A-27). State appropriations that end up as basic income for private institutions as a percentage of appropriations for public institutions, averaged across the United States, are now approximately 4.3 percent (*Supplement,* A-28). On a per full-time student basis, the figure is 13.6 percent.[2]

Forms of support. Almost one-half of the states now give direct support to private institutions. Combining general aid to private institutions and aid to students attending private institutions, about two thirds of all states have programs of support. The highest state, when these two sources are combined and are calculated on a per student basis, is Alaska (Figure 29). When all programs of all sorts are put together, only seven states have no support in any form for private institutions and one of them, Wyoming, has no private institutions (*Supplement,* A-29). All of the remaining six have relatively low enrollments in private institutions.

There are many ways in which states can aid private institutions and the possible combinations among these methods are

---

[1]H. R. Bowen and W. J. Minter, *Private Higher Education* (Washington, D.C.: Association of American Colleges, 1975).

[2]Full-time-equivalent enrollments in private institutions are 32 percent of those in public institutions.

almost limitless (*Supplement,* Section C). The major methods, however, are as follows:

- General-purpose grants to all qualifying institutions—on an enrollment basis, or on the basis of numbers of graduates, as in the case of the "Bundy" plan in New York.
- Grants to specifically identified institutions, such as to the University of Pennsylvania.
- Grants for specific programs, such as to the University of Miami medical school or to dental schools in Michigan.
- Aid to students, such as the scholarship programs in New York and California (open also to students attending public institutions).
- Aid with construction, such as the authority to issue tax-exempt bonds (Michigan), loans for building renovation (New York), and facilities-construction grants (Maryland).
- Extension of tax-exempt privileges of public institutions to private institutions, such as the Pennsylvania exemption from sales and gasoline taxes.
- Limited credits for individuals and corporations for contributions to private colleges, as in Indiana.

The basic issue over state support for private institutions is no longer so much whether it should be undertaken at all, but, rather, how it should be supplied and to what degree. We have made suggestions on these matters in Section 1.

Figure 27. Diversity in the private sector

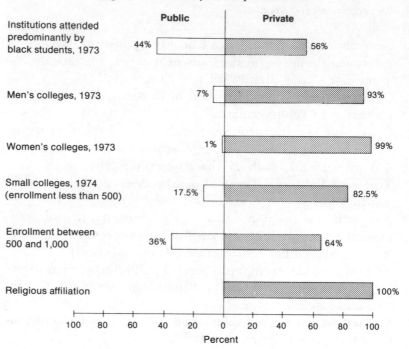

Source: *Supplement*, A-24.

Figure 28. Enrollment in private institutions and enrollment in
private institutions as a percentage of total enrollment, fall enrollment,
1929 to 1975

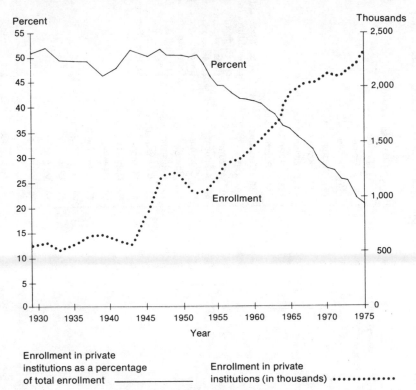

Enrollment in private
institutions as a percentage
of total enrollment ————————

Enrollment in private
institutions (in thousands) ••••••••••••

Sources: *1929-1945:* Enrollment: U.S. Bureau of the Census, *Historical Statistics of the United States, Colonial Times to 1957* (Washington, D.C.: U.S. Government Printing Office, 1961). Percent private: U.S. Office of Education, *Biennial Survey of Education in the United States* (Washington, D.C.: U.S. Government Printing Office, 1940, 1942, 1944, 1946). *1947-1973:* Enrollment: National Center for Education Statistics, *Digest of Educational Statistics, 1974* (Washington, D.C.: U.S. Government Printing Office, 1975), p. 75. *1974-75: Chronicle of Higher Education,* December 16, 1974, and December 15, 1975.

Figure 29. State aid per full-time-equivalent student enrolled in private institutions, 1974-75 (includes aid to students in private institutions and general institutional support of private institutions, arrayed in descending order of aid)

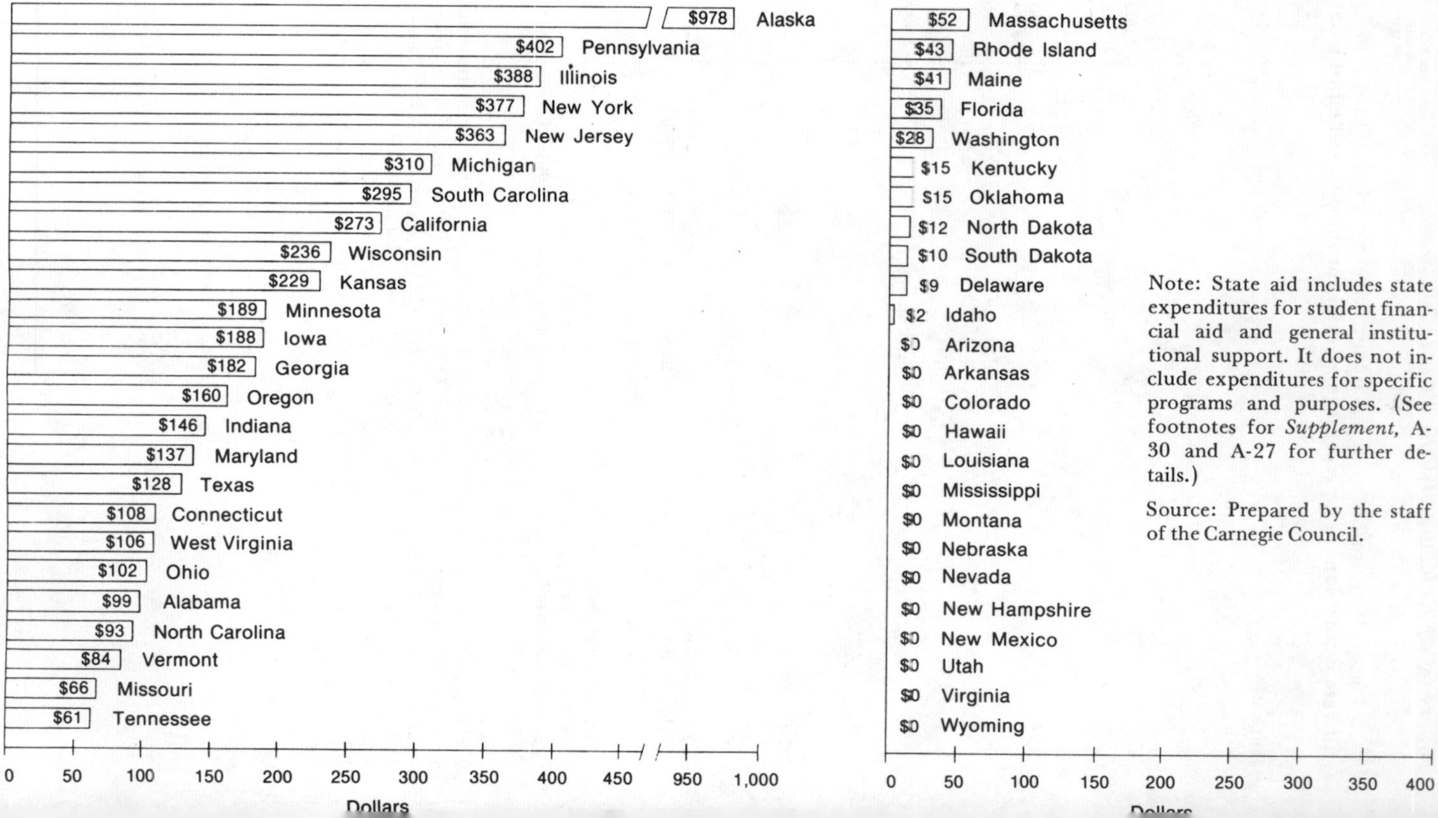

$978 Alaska
$402 Pennsylvania
$388 Illinois
$377 New York
$363 New Jersey
$310 Michigan
$295 South Carolina
$273 California
$236 Wisconsin
$229 Kansas
$189 Minnesota
$188 Iowa
$182 Georgia
$160 Oregon
$146 Indiana
$137 Maryland
$128 Texas
$108 Connecticut
$106 West Virginia
$102 Ohio
$99 Alabama
$93 North Carolina
$84 Vermont
$66 Missouri
$61 Tennessee
0 50 100 150 200 250 300 350 400 450 950 1,000
Dollars
$52 Massachusetts
$43 Rhode Island
$41 Maine
$35 Florida
$28 Washington
$15 Kentucky
$15 Oklahoma
$12 North Dakota
$10 South Dakota
$9 Delaware
$2 Idaho
$0 Arizona
$0 Arkansas
$0 Colorado
$0 Hawaii
$0 Louisiana
$0 Mississippi
$0 Montana
$0 Nebraska
$0 Nevada
$0 New Hampshire
$0 New Mexico
$0 Utah
$0 Virginia
$0 Wyoming
0 50 100 150 200 250 300 350 400

Note: State aid includes state expenditures for student financial aid and general institutional support. It does not include expenditures for specific programs and purposes. (See footnotes for *Supplement*, A-30 and A-27 for further details.)

Source: Prepared by the staff of the Carnegie Council.

7

Diversity of Coordination and Regulation

Coordination, regulation, and consolidation of higher education have been increasing rapidly at the state level. The free-standing campus, uncoordinated and unregulated and unconsolidated with other institutions, once the standard model, is increasingly a rarity in the public sector of higher education.

In 1940, 33 states had no coordinating or planning or consolidating mechanisms covering the entire public sector; today, none are without them.

In 1940, there were only two coordinating agencies (one of them, in New York, was regulatory) over public higher education; today there are 28—of which 19 are regulatory.

In 1940, there were no commissions comparable to the present 1202 commissions (*Supplement, Section F*); today they exist in 46 states.

In 1940, 70 percent of public four-year campuses (other than teachers colleges) were governed by their own individual boards; today about 30 percent of all public four-year campuses are so governed.

In 1940, only one state (New York) had some form of planning or coordination or regulation that covered private colleges and universities; today 49 have such arrangements—the one exception is Wisconsin.

Many forces have been at work encouraging the growth of coordination and regulation beyond the campus level:

- Much more money is now spent on higher education and many more students are accommodated than was earlier the situation. Public interest, as a result, has been heightened.
- More intercampus rivalry exists—community colleges *versus* comprehensive colleges and universities *versus* research universities; public campuses *versus* private campuses. In earlier times, there were few community colleges, and the teachers colleges and the universities each had their clearly separate jurisdictions. Also, private colleges were not receiving public aid.
- Federal aid and interests have been added to state aid and interests, and the federal government has both encouraged and, in some cases, insisted upon, statewide mechanisms for distribution of federal funds and for planning purposes.
- Governors and legislatures have larger and more competent staffs now intent on exercising public authority over higher education.

Alternatives. As centralization progresses, three control issues arise:

- *Campus governance.* There are three clear-cut possibilities here for four-year institutions: (I) that each campus have its own board; (II) that each segment (for example, the university segment and the state college segment, or some other combination of campuses) have its own board; and (III) that all campuses and segments be covered by a single board. Only 5 states still follow the first pattern (campus boards); 8, the second (segmental or combination boards); and 22, the third (consolidated boards). There are also 15 states with mixtures of these three approaches, IV (Table 1).[1]
- *Coordination of all public institutions.* There are four alternatives in current practice: (A) no coordination (9 states); (B) coordination by a consolidated board (13 states); (C) coordination by an advisory council (9 states); and (D) coordination by a regulatory agency (19 states) (Table 2).

[1]Community colleges are not included here. Their arrangements are exceedingly complex.

• *Association of the private sector with public policy forma-
tion.* There are five patterns: (*1*) only one state has no state
planning mechanism in which the private sector participates;
(*2*) in eight states, consolidated boards (all but one of which
also act as state 1202 commissions) serve as the major channel for private sector concerns; (*3*) in another eight states,
advisory coordinating councils, all of which also act as 1202
commissions, serve this function; (*4*) in 18 states, regulatory
coordinating boards, all but three of which act as state 1202
commissions, serve as the major channel for the expression of
views by the private sector; finally, (*5*) in 15 states, the state
1202 commissions are either the only statewide board, or are
separate from any other statewide boards and serve as the
principal contact with private institutions (Table 3).

   The combinations and permutations out of the several possibilities in each of these three areas are almost endless. Thus
New York is a II-D-*4* state, Michigan a I-C-*3* state, and Georgia a
III-B-*5* state. (For a listing of the 18 different combinations currently being used by the 50 states see *Supplement,* Section G.
For some organizational charts of some selected states, see *Supplement,* Section H.)

Impacts. With all this experimentation by the 50 states, it cannot yet be shown that any one approach is superior to any
other approach in its "impacts." There is seemingly no known
quantifiable consequence for actual operating results that can
be associated with one or another approach to centralization of
authority—not on tuition policy, not on state funds for research, not on proportionate dependence on private institutions, not on composition of the public sector, not on any other
thus far statistically tested results. There is one possible exception: the more money spent by the state per student, the more
money spent on the bureaucracy that supervises the expenditures of the money.[2]

---

[2]H. Frost, *Correlation Between Certain Characteristics of Statewide Agencies of Higher Education and Selected Indicators of Higher Education,* prepared for the Carnegie Council on Policy Studies in Higher Education, preliminary draft, December 1975. Later data show some association but no

As another crude check of impacts, we matched our evaluations of current state performances in Section 3 with the methods of control operative both in 1965 and 1970 (to allow time for the different mechanisms to have some effect). We found no clear results. We observe, however, that the best state plans for higher education seem to derive out of advisory and regulatory mechanisms, and least of all out of consolidated boards, and that the quality of the plan is the most important factor in coordination.

The record on impacts is still totally inconclusive. The quality of the "process," however, is another test of the mechanisms—and perhaps an equally or more important one—and we have already expressed some opinions about that in Section 1.

The course of movement, in summary, has been in one direction: toward centralization of planning, of coordination, and of control. But the specific paths followed have been many, and the differential operating practices have apparently been largely unrelated to the paths pursued.

---

obvious causal relationships between certain "characteristics" and certain "indicators." For example, states with (1) low expenditure per student, or (2) lesser reliance on universities in their enrollment patterns, or (3) both, tend to have "relatively strong budgetary review capability" in their regulatory agencies (Letter from Ben Lawrence, Director, National Center for Higher Education Management Systems, April 1, 1976).

Table 1. Patterns of campus governance for senior public institutions

I Individual campus boards (5)	II Multicampus boards (8)	III Consolidated boards (22)		IV Mixed pattern (15)
Delaware	California	Alaska	Oregon	Alabama
Kentucky[a]	Connecticut[d]	Arizona	Rhode Island	Arkansas
Michigan[b]	Illinois	Florida	South Dakota	Colorado
Missouri[c]	Louisiana	Georgia	Utah[f]	Indiana
Washington	Minnesota	Hawaii	West Virginia	Maryland
	Nebraska	Idaho	Wisconsin	Massachusetts
	New York	Iowa	Wyoming[g]	New Jersey
	Tennessee	Kansas		New Mexico
		Maine[e]		Ohio
		Mississippi		Oklahoma
		Montana		Pennsylvania
		Nevada		South Carolina
		New Hampshire		Texas
		North Carolina[f]		Vermont
		North Dakota		Virginia

Definitions

I   Individual board governs each public senior institution.

II   Two or more multicampus boards govern all public senior institutions, e.g., separately for universities and for state colleges. (Note: sometimes these boards have jurisdiction over some two-year institutions as well.)

III   All senior public institutions governed by a single consolidated board.

IV   Mixed pattern with individual boards for some senior institutions and multicampus boards for others.

[a]While Kentucky does have separate boards for all senior institutions, the University of Kentucky board also governs 13 two-year colleges.

[b]Michigan is included in Category I because 13 of the 14 senior institutions have separate governing boards. The University of Michigan board, however, governs three campuses of that system.

[c]Missouri is included in Category I because 8 of the 9 senior institutions have separate governing boards. The University of Missouri board, however, governs four campuses of that system.

[d]The University of Connecticut System board is a multicampus board, but it governs only one senior campus and five two-year campuses.

[e]The Maine Maritime Academy is governed by a separate individual board.

[f]Each campus in the multicampus system also has an individual board with powers largely delegated from the central board.

[g]There is only one senior institution in the state.

Sources: N. M. Berve, "Survey of the Structure of State Coordinating Boards and Public Institutional and Multi-campus Governing Boards of Postsecondary Education—as of January 1, 1975," *Higher Education in the States*, 1975, 4 (10); J. L. Zwingle and M. E. Rogers, *State Boards Responsible for Higher Education 1970* (Washington, D.C.: U.S. Government Printing Office, 1972); U.S. National Center for Education Statistics, *Higher Education Directory, 1974-75* (Washington, D.C.: U.S. Government Printing Office, 1975).

Table 2. Patterns of state coordination of all public institutions of higher education

A No overall coordination (9)	B Coordination by consoli- dated board (13)	C Advisory coordination (9)	D Regulatory coordination (19)	
Arizona[a]	Alaska	Alabama	Colorado	Oregon
Delaware	Georgia	Arkansas	Connecticut	Pennsylvania
Florida[a]	Hawaii	California	Indiana	South Carolin
Iowa[a]	Idaho	Maryland	Illinois	Virginia
Kansas[a]	Maine	Michigan	Kentucky	Tennessee
Mississippi[a]	Montana	Minnesota	Louisiana	Texas
Nebraska	Nevada	New Hampshire	Massachusetts	
North Carolina[a]	North Dakota	Washington	Missouri	
Vermont	Rhode Island	Wyoming	New Jersey	
	South Dakota		New Mexico	
	Utah		New York	
	West Virginia		Ohio	
	Wisconsin		Oklahoma	

Definitions
A   No coordination over the entire public sector (1202 Commissions, as *planning* agencies, a
     treated in Table 3 and *Supplement,* Section D).
B   The consolidated board which governs the public sector also coordinates it.
C   Advisory coordinating board which gives advice to both state government and the instit
     tions of higher education.
D   Regulatory coordinating board which has authority in its own right over one or more ir
     portant aspects of the conduct of higher education, such as the right to approve or di
     approve programs present a single consolidated budget for public higher education.

[a]While no statewide coordination exists in these states, the single governing board for senior insti
tutions does, of course, coordinate them.

Sources: N. M. Berve, "Survey of the Structure of State Coordinating Governing Boards and Publ
Institutional and Multi-campus Governing Boards of Postsecondary Education—as of January
1975," *Higher Education in the States,* 1975, 4 (10); J. L. Zwingle and M. E. Rogers, *State Boarc
Responsible for Higher Education 1970* (Washington, D.C.: U.S. Government Printing Offic
1972); U.S. National Center for Education Statistics, *Higher Education Directory, 1974-75* (Was
ington, D.C.: U.S. Government Printing Office, 1975).

Table 3. Patterns of associating the private sector in higher education
to state public policy

1 mecha- ism (1)	*2* Consolidated board (8)	*3* Advisory council (8)	*4* Regulatory board (18)	*5* Separate 1202 Commis- sion (15)
sconsin	Hawaii	Arkansas[b]	Colorado	Alabama
	Idaho	California	Connecticut	Alaska
	Montana	Maryland[b]	Illinois	Arizona
	North Carolina[a]	Michigan	Indiana	Delaware
	North Dakota	Minnesota	Louisiana	Florida
	Rhode Island	New Hampshire	Massachusetts[b]	Georgia
	Utah	Washington	Missouri	Iowa
	West Virginia	Wyoming	New Jersey[b]	Kansas
			New Mexico	Kentucky
			New York[c]	Maine
			Ohio	Mississippi
			Oklahoma	Nebraska
			Oregon	Nevada
			Pennsylvania[b]	South Dakota
			South Carolina[b]	Vermont
			Tennessee	
			Texas	
			Virginia	

initions
1   No direct contacts with statewide planning (excludes specialized agencies such as scholar-ship commissions).
2   The consolidated governing board which coordinates all public institutions in the state also acts as the channel for private sector concerns, by acting with augmented membership (except Idaho) as the 1202 Commission.
3   Advisory coordinating board also serves as 1202 Commission, and is the channel for private sector concerns.
4   Regulatory coordinating board serves as a major channel for private sector concerns, and, except in Texas where the 1202 Commission is separate and in Colorado and Tennessee which have no 1202 Commissions, the coordinating board also serves as the 1202 Commission.
5   State 1202 Commission acts as a major channel for voicing private sector concerns. In this category the 1202 Commission is either separate from any other statewide board or is the only statewide board.

orth Carolina requires two qualifications to fit this category: there is no 1202 Commission and governing board covers only all public senior institutions. But this board has been given statu-y jurisdiction to consider private sector concerns.

ard is augmented in membership to serve as 1202 Commission.

e New York State Board of Regents by state law has authority over private higher education ich goes far beyond the normal regulatory coordinating board or 1202 Commission relationship.

rces: N. M. Berve, "Survey of the Structure of State Coordinating Governing Boards and Public itutional and Multi-campus Governing Boards of Postsecondary Education—as of January 1, '5," *Higher Education in the States,* 1975, 4 (10); J. L. Zwingle and M. E. Rogers, *State Boards ponsible for Higher Education 1970* (Washington, D.C.: U.S. Government Printing Office, '2); U.S. National Center for Education Statistics, *Higher Education Directory, 1974-75* (Wash-on, D.C.: U.S. Government Printing Office, 1975).

Index